SHINE ON

A great deal of history is about the little cosmic (or maybe more appropriately, "Kosmic") "accidents" that happen along the way. As you will discover in these pages, there are many such episodes from the 100 years of the little brewery in Shiner. As I began this book and started timidly approaching the subject of what to call this thing, another of those little "accidents" happened. One of the first things I jotted down was the phrase, "Shine On." I thought it had a nice sound and represents the attitude of the people, who down through the years have kept our favorite beer flowing.

A little research sealed the deal. Turns out, "Shine On, Harvest Moon" was, for a time, the number one song in the country in 1909, the year the Shiner Brewing Association got its start.

I took that as an endorsement from up on high and immediately quit my title search. Here's hoping you agree with my decision.

AN ADMISSION

I am not a historian. Never claimed to be one. I am, however, a lover of beer and fan of history. That said and out of the way, my task here is to tell a story. In doing that and trying to keep you interested, I've, no doubt, left out lots of details and facts. I beg your forgiveness for any such omissions which may lie near and dear to your heart and ask only that you understand any such occurrence is not the result of malice nor slovenliness, but only due to the limitations of space, both in this book and in my rather over-cluttered mind.

CHORUS OF
"SHINE ON, HARVEST MOON"
BY
JACK NORWORTH AND NORA BAYES

Oh, shine on, shine on, harvest moon
Up in the sky;
I ain't had no lovin'
Since January, February, June or July.
Snow time ain't no time to stay
Outdoors and spoon;
So shine on, shine on, harvest moon,
For me and my gal.

WELCOME

SHI

CLEANEST LI

TO

NER

TLE CITY

IN TEXAS

1909

Shiner Brewery
Shiner Texas

SHINE ON

★ ★

100 YEARS OF HISTORY, LEGENDS, HALF-TRUTHS AND TALL TALES ABOUT TEXAS' MOST BELOVED LITTLE BREWERY.

BRIGHT SKY PRESS

2365 RICE BOULEVARD

HOUSTON, TEXAS 77005

10   9   8   7   6   5   4   3   2   1

Library of Congress Cataloging-in Publication Data

Renfro, Mike.

Shine On: 100 Years of Shiner Beer / by Mike Renfro.

p. cm.

ISBN 978-1-933979-20-5 (hbk. : alk. paper)

1. Shiner Brewing Association – History.

2. Beer industry – Texas – Shiner – History.

3. Breweries – Texas – Shiner – History.

4. Shiner (Tex.) – History.

I. Title.

HD9397.U54S557 2008

338.7'6634209764—dc22

2008027804

Book and cover design by Ryan Rhodes, McGarrah Jessee, Inc.

Printed in China

CONTENTS

K. SPOETZL BREWERY

Spoetzl Brewery — Shiner, Texas.

FOREWORD

MIKE RENFRO

I f you are well and truly blessed in this life, you may someday find yourself living in an era well beyond that of your birth. And if you are blessed even further, you will find yourself walking deftly through that time while retaining the grace of the years of your youth.

My grandmother was such a person. Living to just five years shy of her centennial year, she spoke in a more melodic, graceful fashion that has been lost to modern English. Like a thoughtfully written letter salvaged from an old attic, she used phrases like "we commenced to laughing," and "in the course of time, we realized our lot was elsewhere." In her later years, she fell into the tendency of telling many of the same stories over and over, but like a great song, I wanted to hear them again just for the music that accompanied the lyrics.

At the same time, she carried a wit and understanding of these present times that served her well. Until her voluntary retirement in 1992 from driving without incident and—I might add—a driver's license, she negotiated town in a yacht-sized 1960 Pontiac Catalina that served her purposes but looked as foreign as a Fiat in Dalhart. Once, during the final years of her once-a-week trip to the grocery store, the teenager loading her groceries in the massive trunk stared at the great white beast incredulously and asked, "Ma'am, what year model is this thing?" She replied without missing a beat, "Why, honey, it's a 1990 model, can't you tell?"

Without question, she was of another time, but well and fully at home in this one.

It occurs to me that the Spoetzl Brewery, though nine years her junior, is much like that fine lady.

Ours is a pre-fab, tear-it-down-if-it's-old, corporate outsourcing kind of world. But even amongst all that, our lives are occasionally brightened by someone or something that remains un-strip-malled and genericized.

Kosmos Spoetzl wouldn't recognize the times and places in which we find ourselves, but he would recognize his beer, his brewery and his town. Some of the faces there today carry unmistakable resemblances to faces he knew and employed.

And for a 100-year-old, Shiner Beer and The Spoetzl Brewery are doing just fine, thank you. Like my grandmother did for so many decades, Shiner's not only survived, but also thrived. Blessed with the good genes of its Czech and German parents, Shiner's more popular today than ever before, ably changing and innovating where needed, but never forgetting who they are.

In the following pages, I will do my best to recount Shiner's life story and tell you a little about all the great people who've made that story what it is. Like any life, it's been filled with ups and downs and lots of good friends.

So pull up a chair, grab a cold Shiner out of the fridge and have a seat.

Have I got a story for you.

CHAPTER 1

THEY LEFT
EVERYTHING
BEHIND
BUT THE
BEER

1800's – EARLY 1900's

Just for grins, turn the air conditioning off for a few days. Throw away your bug spray, all sunscreen and don't pay your electric bill for a while. Cut off virtually all contact with friends and family and give a large sum of money to a group of strangers to take you out into the middle of nowhere and summarily dump you.

Next, resolve to live among unfriendly natives, scorpions and all manner of snakes on hard ground that is prone to drought, flood, fire, and pretty much every scourge and weather severity known to man.

Mix thoroughly with a dash of hindsight and a hearty serving of homesickness and you've got yourself a taste of what the first German and Czech immigrants to Texas encountered upon arrival.

Given all that they faced, you can easily see why one of their highest priorities—once the basic questions of survival were dealt with, anyway—was to figure out a way to brew some beer. More than just taking the edge off an otherwise harsh reality, it was a taste of home. They weren't on some grand mission to bring the traditions of Old World brewing to the wilds of Texas; it was just about survival first.

Second, there was the remembering. Whether it was the old country, family left behind, or just the right way to do things, the beer was that remembered thing that made the surviving worthwhile in a world otherwise turned on its ear.

And just maybe, looking back at that very hard world from a considerably softer vantage point, those first few teeth-rattling years on that road known as the immigrant experience in Texas are what gave Shiner its strong constitution.

Fact is, we nearly lost the old brewery on more than a couple of occasions. And while there are no quantifiable scientific facts that can be cited as evidence, it's hard not to believe that those first few years of the surviving and the remembering didn't somehow wedge itself into the Shiner DNA.

So at the end of the day, it all goes back to the immigrants, who, at the end of their day, were determined to enjoy a good beer.

Their formula worked.

Still does.

Common sense, of course, would have dictated that the Germans and Czechs never would have come here at all. It was a far distant existence, not just in sheer miles, but in geography, weather and pretty much everything else you can think of. Of course, common sense, for all its value, never dictated much of what we call history. On the contrary, from the very beginning, most leaps of faith were perceived by a goodly number of people as exercises in futility. Our planet's still full of shipwrecks, massacre sites and battlefields bearing testament to those leaps of faith that came to bad ends.

But for every dozen or two that didn't quite work out, there's the occasional big payoff. Lewis and Clark were idiots when they left and heroes when they returned. The Wright Brothers ended up not being so peculiar after all, and a good number of the dreamers who packed up in Bavaria, unsure of where they'd be unpacking, did all right as well.

The ironic thing is, advertising—a pretty much indispensable part of modern beer marketing—played a huge role in getting those first brave/crazy souls here in the first place. Granted, it was a decidedly 19th century form of advertising, devoid of stunning special effects or Super Bowl extravaganzas, but it was advertising nonetheless.

Prior to 1831, there were few Germans living in Texas. When Friedrich Ernst moved to Austin County from Oldenburg, Germany, he found the land so much to his liking he wrote a very enthusiastic letter to friends back home. Eventually, the letter was published in a German newspaper, creating enough interest to bring the first few trickles across the ocean to Galveston, thence north and west from there. The tracks of the influx can still be seen today with a glance at a Texas map and the location of the towns they settled.

But if Ernst's letter was the advertising campaign that set the exodus in motion, the sweepstakes promotion that really got everybody worked up was the *Verein*.

The *Verein* was a society of wealthy Germans who wanted to purchase land in Texas, then sell it to immigrants. Their motivations were both philanthropic and economic, but in either case, marketing and advertising would play a big role.

Of course, advertising, as anyone who's ever bought a 99-cent hamburger will tell you, can be prone to overpromise, and such was the case with the *Verein*.

They offered free transportation to the colony, free land once there, and all the tools and provisions (on credit) necessary to begin farming on the new land. Upon the harvest of the second successive crop, the debt would be repaid to the *Verein*.

There was just one small problem, one that these days would probably be addressed through fine print or a ridiculously fast-talking announcer.

The colony the *Verein* intended to settle, known as the Fisher-Miller Grant, was not actually theirs to sell. It was also located in west-central Texas, well west of any area of

rivers, thence fanning out along the path to the ill-fated colony.

The Czechs, too, had their pied piper. Evangelist, you might even say. In 1849, the Reverend Josef Arnost Bergmann left his Czech homeland and set out on the arduous 17-week voyage to Galveston. Given that the land he was to settle was actually reachable and farmable, he too wrote a very enthusiastic letter back to his homeland, extolling the virtues of his new life in Texas. The local paper in his hometown, *Moravské Noviny* (*Moravian News*), published his letter as well.

The results were similar to the German story. Given less than optimum times in the region, a flood of the wide-eyed and hopeful set out on the brutal voyage to Galveston, Indianola and points beyond in Texas. Some brought their accordions and still others brought their brewing skills. Pretty much all of them brought their appreciation of both of those things.

Given their original geographical proximity to the Germans, it only makes sense that in their new home, old differences would seem less problematic. They settled in relatively close proximity to one another, and, in some cases, in the same towns, happy to see faces at least from the same continent as

Fact is, we nearly lost the old brewery on more than a couple of occasions.

rainfall suitable to farming and, worse, the grant lay upon rocky soils favored by no one outside of some very jealous Comanche Indians.

Fact of the matter was, Prince Carl von Solms-Braunfels, Baron von Meusebach and the other members of the *Verein* had never actually seen the land to which they were dispatching so many of their countrymen. And in the end, neither did any of those who bought into the plan. The towns of New Braunfels and Fredericksburg were about as far as any of them ever made it, though those towns were intended merely as way stations along the route to the promised land, lying another 80 or 100 miles to the northwest.

Much like a more modern-day swampland development, the *Verein* eventually folded, leaving more than a few families holding onto worthless deeds and dear life in a very forbidding place. Even Indianola, the port town along the Gulf of Mexico where many of the immigrants first set foot on Texas soil, was eventually wiped off the face of the map by a hurricane.

Without the resources to return to the old country, they settled in the swath, roughly between the Colorado and Brazos

that from which they had originated.

As it turned out, the Germans and Czechs weren't the only ones glad to see one another and willing to forget former differences. Evidence of that fact lives on even now throughout Texas. Mexicans living in the same region, given similarly to a love of music and cold beer, adopted the Czech and German instrument of choice, the accordion, as their own and blended it into their music.

What we today call "Norteno" or "Conjunto" (all together) music is still liberal in the use of the accordion. San Antonio stands as the biggest example of a city cobbled together out of the rich mix of the Bohemian and Mexican cultures. But the state is surprisingly rife with smaller towns that still bear the unmistakable mark of Czech and German influence. Fredericksburg, New Braunfels, West, and, of course, Shiner.

In all of these towns, there are the older ones who still speak at least bits and pieces of the old tongue. In some cases there still are radio stations broadcasting in German and Czech, there are kolaches, and oompah bands, and, in Shiner, there is the beer.

Ah, yes, that little detail.

Sitting right in the middle of that swath of settlements that spread out from Galveston west to San Antonio, New Braunfels and Fredericksburg, Shiner was originally known as "Half Moon," Texas. The coming of the railroad to a site near this community but not right through it, could have meant the death of the town as it did for many others in Texas, but the folks who'd chosen their lot there were more industrious than that. If the railroad wouldn't come to them, by God, they figured they'd just pick up and move to the railroad. A large parcel of land owned by cattleman and businessman Henry Shiner was where they needed to be. Said land was graciously donated to the enterprise and, as his reward, Mr. Shiner had the whole town named in his honor.

It's not known whether he was a teetotaler or not, but surely he'd be amused to know he also ended up with a beer named after him as well. That, and the fact his act of generosity would be repaid millions of times over in the future by virtue of his name traveling from coast to coast, courtesy of the label on a brown longneck bottle.

nearby was good, but not good enough. Maybe the thought was that they'd endured enough during their trek across the ocean and it wasn't too much to ask to have a beer exactly to their liking, given the fact so many other things had been strange and requiring some getting used to in this land.

Thus, in 1909, The Shiner Brewing Association got *its* start. But if you're going to brew beer, you need a brewmaster, and so the farmers and businessmen in the association made a deal with Mr. Herman Weiss of Galveston whereby he would move his family and his brewing equipment to Shiner to manage the brewery. In June of 1909, the brewing association began boring a water well, which hit artesian water at a depth of only 55 feet. If the association needed a sign, they had it. By July, the appropriate government officials had inspected and blessed the site, next to Boggy Creek and the all-important railroad tracks, and Shiner keg beer was soon on sale in every saloon in Shiner and surrounding towns.

One small problem. Conditions weren't always ideal in the old brewery building, nor in the monetary stores of the association. "Quality issues," as they euphemistically say, plagued the

---

The irony, of which there are many concerning this story, is that most people even today don't know that Shiner is not just a beer, but a town, let alone the fact that before it was ever a town, it was a person.

The irony, of which there are many concerning this story, is that most people even today don't know that Shiner is not just a beer, but a town, let alone the fact that before it was ever a town, it was a person. Regardless, Henry Shiner's gift of land along the railroad tracks began to grow and prosper. In the late 19th century, cotton was the main source of wealth, grown in the rich soils and shipped out along the all-important steel lifeline. The rails also served to bring in those things necessary to life—particularly the German and Czech immigrant life—which, of course, had to include beer. It came from Galveston or San Antonio and did the job of quenching thirsts, but something was missing.

Maybe this is where the term "local flavor" got its start, but whatever the case, the locals had a decidedly do-it-yourself gene in their being that led them to form—like other groups might form task forces or civic committees—the Shiner Brewing Association. Most of the folks around town were farmers of one kind or another, not far removed from that other world across the ocean, and beer from other places

struggling enterprise. If you've ever had a soured beer, you've experienced a "quality issue" and know how unpleasant such an encounter can be. Apparently, a number of people during those early years endured that very experience. But more than upturned noses and bad faces, this led to the brewery nearly going bankrupt on two occasions.

And like any football team in any town in Texas that doesn't win enough, the association went in search of a new coach. The stars aligned and, thus, who else could have been right for the job other than a sickly man with the name of "Kosmos"?

Just like most of the rest of the immigrants to the area, he never really intended to be here in the first place. Kosmos Spoetzl was born March 3, 1873 (one day after Texas Independence Day) in the town of Rosenheim, in Bavaria. In time, he attended brewmaster's school and eventually migrated to Cairo, Egypt, to head the appropriately named Pyramid Brewery. Kosmos had health problems, though, and was advised to leave Egypt. In a case of going from one extreme to the other, he took a job in Saskatchewan. In what must

LEFT: Were it not for Henry B. Shiner, you might be drinking something called "Half Moon Beer" these days. Just doesn't have quite the same ring to it, does it?

MR. HENRY B. SHINER
FOUNDER OF THE CITY OF SHINER
PICTURE TAKEN IN 1875

surely have been a case of extreme culture shock, he and his wife were to take a dog sled from Montreal to his new job site. But while waiting for that to happen, he became ill (a cold, maybe?) and ended up being hospitalized for several months.

Around this time, some genius of the medical profession suggested a warmer climate without so much sand, and they made a move to San Francisco. Trouble was, it was only a couple of years after the great earthquake of 1906. Though there was much rebuilding and construction work to be had, the breweries had either yet to be put back in working order or were simply not hiring.

For what little odd jobs or laborer positions there might have been, Kosmos was patently overqualified. He'd grown up in the cradle of beer civilization and had been around the business his entire life. Through his years of study, apprenticeship and at the helm of Pyramid, he'd developed a recipe, the details of which only he and a very select few others would ever fully know. Yet circumstance seemed determined to keep what he was convinced was the best formulation of beer ever, from making its way from his mind into a frosty mug.

The stars aligned, and thus, who else could have been right for the job other than a sickly man with the name of Kosmos.

He kept his chin up (actually, chins up) about things, though. He was always a cheerful man, fond of kids and anyone who'd listen to him talk about what made for good beer. Matter of fact, about the only thing that could get him red-faced and crossing back and forth between German and English words not generally considered usable in polite company, was any slight of the brewer's art or indifference to a greatly crafted beer. Even if he happened to see you drinking a glass of water, he'd good-naturedly lay into you.

"Waz wit dis vater you're drinking?" he'd demand. "Zee vater is for washing your feet, beer is for drinking. Here, I get you vun."

Suffice it to say, the bottled and designer water craze of the last 15 or so years would most likely have set him off. Nor is it hard to imagine the sound of him on a lengthy and only partly comprehendible diatribe regarding beer versus water and the missed opportunities inherent with the overconsumption of water not blended with barley, hops and yeast.

Some men were painters, or sculptors, maybe engineers, chefs or soldiers. Kosmos Spoetzl was a little of all of those things, and beer was as much a work of art as anything you could find on a canvas. It certainly took a lot of knowledge from a lot of different disciplines, and by damn, it was certainly worth fighting for. San Francisco was not to be his battlefield, though. The town simply wasn't back to its old self yet.

He had, during the course of his stay there, become aware of a couple of breweries in San Antonio, Texas. Yes, the weather, he was told, could certainly be hot, but not in the gritty desert-like way of Cairo. His research on the city offered further encouragement in that there was a substantial German population in and around the area, and in light of this, certainly there must be a deep appreciation for an authentic beer made the way they did it in the old country.

Apparently, the weather agreed with him more than that in Cairo and Montreal, and Kosmos and his wife decided to stay. While there, he worked as an assistant brewmaster and tried to figure out what to do with his future. After some months, he heard tell of a little town a few miles to the east where they liked beer and those who knew how to brew it. The fact they spoke his language was just gravy. He made a trip to check it out, and the rest, well...let's just say, what happened after that is the kind of thing you could write a book about.

After five years of limping along, The Shiner Brewing Association felt like they'd found the man who could get things on track. The big man with the tilted hat, waistcoat and ever-present cigar who rolled into town that first day was clearly not just someone looking for a job. From the first moment hands were shaken and introductions were made, it was as if an evangelist had ridden into town ready to relay the good news to all who would come to his tent. And in spite of the cordial and humble way he greeted all who came to show him around that day, there was a certain cockiness inside. He could show these people what real beer was. He could bring them something Cairo, Montreal, San Francisco, and even the great towns of Bavaria couldn't have.

Don't get me wrong here. There was not an ounce of palpable arrogance in Kosmos Spoetzl. Anyone who ever met him will confirm that. But like any great musician or athlete or anyone particularly good at what they do, there is the belief

TOUGH CROWD: This is what passed for "consumer research" back in the day. And if they didn't like something, they'd let you know.

STANDING FROM LEFT: Guston Schmidt, unidentified, August Schramm, unidentified, unidentified, Frederich Pfuhl, Fritz Rogge, Max Woelters, Gottlieb Helweg, unidentified, John Niemeyer. SITTING FROM LEFT: Carl Draeger, William Zander, Lou Pfaeules, Louis Ehlers, J.H. Huebner, Rev. Dziewas, unidentified, Dietrich Othold, unidentified, Bill Wendtland, William Hagendorf

LET'S HOPE THERE WAS NO FIRE AFTER THIS WAS TAKEN: The fire department does their part to save water, much to the liking of Kosmos.

inside that "what I do, nobody else can do." Sure, you can *call* it arrogance if you want to, but given the roadblocks he'd managed to climb over to get to Shiner, Texas, from the other side of the world, sheer belief in what he was doing and the rightness of it seems a more apt description.

The men of the brewery association could certainly see something in him anyway. In November 1914, the association leased the brewery to Kosmos. He immediately started some renovations and by the end of January 1915, he began brewing Old World Bavarian beer from that recipe he carried everywhere. It was, for the most part, one that had been handed down through several generations of his family. That was the part he would tell you about. The other part, the most important part of the recipe, was his own little twist on what the previous generations had done. That part never got put down on paper. It rode comfortably up under the crown of Kosmos' slightly tilted hat. The joke was, that's what made his hat always ride his head that way, there being a big lump wherein the particulars of the recipe resided.

The original recipe for that bottle sitting in front of you involved a whole lot more than barley, hops, artesian water and the like. There was, of course, what the immigrant carried around in his head. Then, too, there was a whole lot of flavor thrown in over those years between Bavaria and Shiner. There was sickness, there was uncertainty and there was the determination that, somewhere, there existed the place that his beer was meant for.

The portly little German man with the hat was the secret ingredient that—once added to the wonderful Czech-German mishmash of humanity already in place—allowed the all-important aging process to begin.

They may have lived a long time ago in a world very different from the one we know. It's next to impossible to imagine what their life was like or the way they coped with all they faced. And try as you might, you will never fully get inside their heads. But when it comes right down to it, the one thing we can fully understand and get our considerably softer hands around, is the love of a good beer.

And as for water...well...you know what you can do with that.

B9897   Shiner Brewery, Shiner, Texas

ABOVE: The beginning,
circa 1909.

RIGHT: Making beer
is serious business:
Apparently filling kegs
is never as much fun as
emptying them.

OSHA WOULDA HAD A FIELD DAY: The old tin brewhouse was no place for the careless.

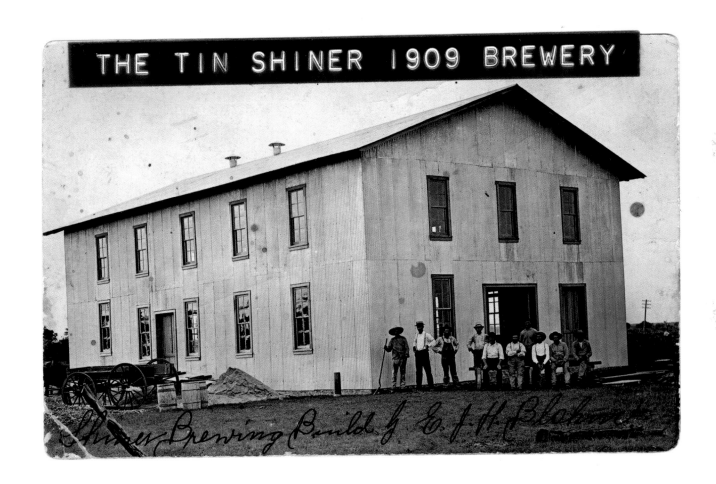

THE TIN SHINER 1909 BREWERY

Shiner Brewing Build g E. J. H. Blahm

LEFT: Kosmos and crew working hard to get things flowing.

ABOVE: If you build it, they will drink: The construction of the old tin brewhouse in 1909.

ABOVE: The Opera House
Saloon was always full of
those looking to escape the
Texas heat.

RIGHT: No fighting, no spitting,
leave your guns at the door:
One of the local Shiner drinking
establishments.

CHAPTER 2

A COLD SHINER ON A FENCE POST

1909 — 1919

There's a big patch of grass out in front of the old brewery, occupied by a few cedar elm trees and a white frame house. It's what greets you when you pull down the road for the brewery tour. Sometimes they barbecue out there on a Friday.

It's not all manicured, corporately cropped and flowered like you might expect a ride through the gates of one of the mega-brewers to be. Things look kept, but not overkept. If it's the fall, when the humidity's broken some, it's the kind of place you can lay back, pull up a piece of shade and take a siesta. Depending on the wind, you may hear the rhythmic clinking of the longnecks on the bottling line or maybe a Union Pacific freight rolling through, but you can get a nap in after lunch if you want. And if the cicadas are still hanging on a little bit, so much the better.

You will not be prodded by a rent-a-cop dispatched from the main security gate, because there isn't one. The day I did this, the folks at Spoetzl did not know me from Adam but were fine with my impromptu enjoyment of the brewery grounds—a pair of words which somehow seems too official and cold for this little plot of grass and trees out in front of a building that looks way smaller than you thought it would be before you came here.

If anybody had noticed, they might have thought I'd spent too much time in the Hospitality Room. In fact, at that point, I hadn't even been in there. Or gone on the tour, or eaten barbecue in the break room with folks who have nicknames like Tool Box and Redbird (a lady) and a half-dozen or so of the other people who keep on doing what this place has kept on doing since 1909.

I wanted to listen to what the place had to say before I did any talking or asked any dumb writer questions.

Between the breeze blowing through the trees and the little white house that still stands right across from the brewery, I figured I could encounter a ghost or two. Or at least a feeling. And failing all that, then at least a good 20 minutes of shut-eye.

If I had gotten out to this little patch 70 or 80 years earlier, there would have been sheep out there. Kosmos always kept 'em. It's one of the first things the older ones who still

remember him from their childhoods will tell you. I suspect it was part German utilitarianism—sheep being a good way to keep the grass mowed—and, on the aesthetic side, not at all unpleasant to look at.

The sheep, like Kosmos, are all gone now.

Or are they?

Actually, the flock shows up every weekday a little before the 11 or 1:30 brewery tours. This kind wears T-shirts, biker vests, ripped jeans, tennis shoes and sometimes boots. And maybe when you think about it, sheep is the last thing you should call them, as they are not followers of the beer behemoths of Milwaukee or St. Louis but of their own path. Their devotion to Kosmos' enterprise being enough to cause them to pack up the car and make the trek from Austin or Houston, or Englewood, New Jersey, or Hamburg, Germany or...

Pilgrims maybe?

As I understand it, Mohammed left the building a long time ago in Mecca but that doesn't stop a few kagillion Muslims from descending on the place every year, not to see him, but to walk in the same place, touch the stuff he touched. Put a smell and a feel to someone you've only encountered in ink and through stories up to now.

Yeah, pilgrims.

Maybe an overly grand term in regards to beer, but I guess, on that fall day, I was a pilgrim too. I wasn't here for the free beer, though I rarely refuse one. I was looking for Kosmos or, at the very least, a trace of him. Maybe, buried in the dirt, one of the nickels he used to keep in his pocket to give to any kid he saw.

"An old man with a metal detector and some time on his hands could probably do pretty well out here," I thought to myself.

I suppose I figured I'd find something of him out amongst the trees and the grass because while old Kosmos was by title a brewmaster, some of his best work was done without benefit of a roof over his head, or apron around his considerable waist.

At least that's the way it was for most of the years he ran this place. After his initial leasing and later purchase of the Shiner Brewing Association, he had immediately gone to work fixing what was broken, putting in some new equipment and generally making the adjustments that would be necessary to brew his Old World Bavarian beer. Those first few months were frantic and pivotal. Glowing yellowish light, via either bulb or candle, depending on the still-iffy electrical supply, glowed long into the night through the windows of the brewery. That curious new man from Bavaria by way of Cairo, Canada, San Francisco and San Antonio, et al, was up to something.

Liken it, if you will, to a teenage kid buying an old classic car that needs a heck of a lot of work. Months of lying under an incontinent oil pan and enduring the fangs of unseen things under the alternator are tolerated in anticipation of that moment when he can finally get his dream out of the garage and cruise around town for all to see.

Actually, there's more truth to that comparison than you might think.

Kosmos Spoetzl, having gotten things up to snuff inside the brewery, realized that the locals probably still didn't quite know what to think of him, so he took his new baby out for a spin—literally. "Field research," you might call it.

ride down any local road was punctuated by row after row of cotton bolls and, more often than not, the farmers or hired help whose backbreaking job it was to maintain and pick it. Not only was it hard work, it was hot work.

Kosmos would head out each day about half-past heatstroke in the afternoon and drive by the fields. A lot of times, they saw him coming, the cloud of dust rising up over the tree line in the distance and giving them enough time to walk over to

No, Texas wasn't heaven on earth, but it was a good place to brew both a beer and a life.

He bought a Model T, outfitted the back to accommodate a couple of kegs and the appropriate amount of ice, then hit the pavement—or, as it was at this time, the dirt. He'd drive the country roads around Shiner with his jolly cargo. Something akin to an ice cream man for those of legal drinking age (though said age was highly elastic at that time). As far as can be determined, there wasn't recorded polka music blaring from a roof-mounted speaker, though you must admit it would have been a nice touch. Doubtless, the killjoys and nannies that suck the oxygen out of our modern world would have a thing or two to say about Kosmos' idea of beer distribution. But things were slower then, and that included the now-long-reaching tentacles of those who would save us from our own judgments.

As it was in 1915, cotton, not the killjoys, occupied every spare inch of dirt on the fertile soils of Lavaca County, and a

the edge of the road and get a big sweaty, red-cheeked smile and a cold beer. Usually, a bit of small talk, sometimes in German, sometimes in his heavily-accented English, always heavily peppered with laughter and the smoke from his ever-present cigar.

Plenty of times through the years, he'd pass a field where the farmer was plowing way over on the other side of the property. Given all the stops he had to make on a typical circuit, time was limited, so Kosmos took to taking a cold bottle of beer and setting it on the nearest fencepost to be retrieved when the farmer got over that way.

Given the heat and severity of the work, he most likely could have set bottles of vinegar or Navidad River water on the fence-posts and still have been received as an angel, as long as the liquid he left was cold.

ABOVE: Cotton Patch. For many years, cotton was king in Shiner. Bales of it could often be seen adjacent to the brewery. This patch was a nod to that. By the 1940's, the cotton was all but gone, though it would be memorialized on every bottle of Shiner Premium.

Add to the hard labor the fact that the boll weevil and overuse of the soils was resulting in rapidly declining cotton harvests, a cold beer—better yet a free cold beer—bought loyalty and appreciation far beyond anything the brewery may have lost in revenues. Some might wish to draw skeptical conclusions from it, but as cotton production continued to go south, Spoetzl's Old Bavarian brew continued to rise in popularity.

Local saloons like the Bismarck, the Aransas Pass, the Palace and the Favorite stocked it and did a good business with it, providing Kosmos and company with much-needed funds to put back in the brewery.

By August of 1915, Kosmos had bought the brewery outright and installed a fine, new large beer vat, capable of holding 335 kegs of beer. This increased the storage capacity of the place to 500 barrels. Though keg beer was the primary way of getting the nectar to the bees, work was also begun on a bottle shop.

Miles and country road dust continued to pile up on the old Model T as Kosmos continued his daily rounds through the cotton fields. The once-sickly man who couldn't seem to find a climate to suit his health now seemed to be doing just fine, thank you, in the heat and humidity on the north edge of the coastal plain. To anyone who ever met him, there was no trace of frailness; in fact, it seemed as if he'd always been there waiting with a good German beer, a grin and a nickel for those not yet of age.

In a rare case of perception and reality lining up neatly and seamlessly, he renamed the brewery, the Home Brewery, as if to say to everyone who cared to notice, that this was where he intended to stay. All those years of never really feeling good, no matter which part of the world he was in, had just been not-so-subtle nudges towards the place he needed to be. No, Texas wasn't heaven on earth, as some of the enthusiastic letters from the early German immigrants had declared all those years before, but it was a good place to brew both a beer and a life.

Charlie Goodnight, the old cattleman, Texas Ranger and subject of the Larry McMurtry novel and TV mini-series *Lonesome Dove,* had done much the same thing with a different commodity. He'd come to Texas with not much of anything and managed to put together some good cattle. Not blessed with the Model T, as Kosmos was, he took the cattle to where they were needed via horseback. He and Oliver Loving's

first drives of longhorn cattle north to where the railroads were is the stuff of much we call the Texas legend, that lives on even now.

Texas has a way of growing those kinds of stories. Charlie Goodnight did it with cattle, Kosmos Spoetzl did it with the thing those cowboys were most thirsty for when they reached Dodge City or Abilene, Kansas—a good, cold beer.

I do not propose to equate the two, but certainly you could agree with me that there were parallels. Both took their product where it was most wanted and, moreover, both faced hardships that would threaten their way of life. The barbed wire that provided the fences upon which Kosmos would leave his gifts in the hot summers of the middle teens was the very thing that spelled the doom of the drives Goodnight and partner Loving pioneered in the 1870s. Goodnight survived by buying up large chunks of the newly fenced ranch lands and making do with the new reality.

So, too, would Kosmos be presented with a new reality that could either be given into, or beaten. As the brewery continued to grow and prosper, war loomed on the very continent Kosmos and so many of his neighbors had come from. The gloomy prospect of Prohibition stood there as well, all forbidding, much closer, and potentially career-ending.

You have to wonder about the thoughts that would go through a man's mind, given such a circumstance after just a taste of success. It would be easy, given all his previous life's hardships, for a man like Kosmos Spoetzl to become embittered and decide he was just not meant to succeed and this was simply the lot life had dealt him. Some in this world do exactly that. Most, one could argue. But legends and books and brands are not built around such people.

Fences.

It hit me right then, as I lay there on the grass outside the old man's brewery that was still brewing all these years later. Fences are what we make of them. Either limitations on what we can accomplish or opportunities to do something nobody else thought to do. He took his fences and turned 'em into coasters upon which a beer could be sat.

Maybe *that's* why he always had the sheep out there. Maybe it was his way of reminding himself that fences served a purpose and could be a good thing, as well as a limitation.

I got up from my comfortable place on the grass outside the brewery and wondered if he'd come out here back in those days and enjoyed the feel of the grass, the warmth of the

RIGHT: You always knew when that Spoetzl fellow had been around.

38

sunshine and the rhythmic reassurance of the cicadas, as I'd been doing.

I was starting to think I'd actually managed to find that little ghost of Kosmos I'd been looking for.

He's still here, even if his sheep aren't.

And as I watched a big group of people make their way in for the 1:30 brewery tour, I realized...

Actually, the flock's bigger than it's ever been.

LEFT: The streets were dusty, but that didn't mean your throat had to be: Downtown Shiner, circa 1915.

ABOVE: Patrons from a local bar in Shiner.

41

RIGHT: Kosmos and two of the ever-present menagerie that could always be found on the grounds.

FAR RIGHT: No place like it; the brewery changed its name to the Home Brewery in 1920.

Shiner Texas Aug 17-13

The Directors of the Home Brewing Co.
met at the Opera House J C Blohm presi=
present were J C Blohm President J H
Huebner, W S Wendtland, M S Wolters
Aug Schramm & J A Berckenhoff
a Motion was made and duly second
to allow J H Huebner 25 Cts on every
quarter of a Barrel to go around the
Saloons Motion Carried.
The following Bills were read and ordered
to be paid Jos. Mikulik $6.05 the
Balance to be paid later. O. G. Blohm
$14.55 Shiner Hardware Co 3.80 Garbade
Lumber Co $14.05 F. W. Heitmann 78.00
having all Business disposed off, Motion
was made to adjourn

J. H Huebner Secty

J C Blohm Pres

BEER BREAK

WHO ARE THESE ARTESIANS AND WHAT IS SO SPECIAL ABOUT THEIR WATER, ANYWAY?

L et's just all admit it up front, "artesian water" is one of those terms that everyone's heard and nobody understands. It's the beer equivalent of "dual overhead cam engine," or "Certified Angus Beef." Everybody says it, everybody hears it and nods their head, but nobody has any idea what the hell any of it means, nor are we likely to since we're all too scared to hold our hands up and admit as much.

I'm as guilty as anybody. Given the fact my eyes are usually bugged over by such things, I just nod my head too. Matter of fact, even though I have owned quite a few cars over the years, it has never interested me in the least if the cams in said car are of the dual variety and whether they are overhead, under my backside or shoved randomly into the glove box with my proof of insurance and owner's manual that I never looked at.

And yes ma'am, I have had way more beers than cars over the years, and though the folks at Shiner just about aquify their pants when I say this, I never gave a whole lot of thought to the origins of the water either, be it the Rockies, the Cascades, the Alleghenies, artesian or the hydrant and hose out behind Big Dave's Paint and Body Shop.

This is my bad.

To make amends, I wish now to explain why you and I should care about artesian water and what it means to beer.

First off, an artesian water well is...well...rare. Such wells are named after the former province of France by the name of Artois. Carthusian monks (I'll spare you the details of who those guys were) first dug them in 1126. Simply put, such a well is the kind where you hit water that shoots to the surface without the need of pumping. To put it in Texas terms, it's like when you drill for oil and hit a gusher.

You, my friend, are in the money. And in sometimes drought-prone climes like Texas, a good, strong, flowing artesian well is, in many ways, every bit as fortunate a strike as the kinds of wells that made J.R. rich in the old *Dallas* TV show.

Then, of course, there are additional purity benefits of the water being filtered through limestone on its way to the surface. Bottom line is: an artesian well says, "You can make it here."

And so it was that in 1909, when the original Shiner Brewing Association drilled for water on the property where the Spoetzl Brewery now sits, it was somewhat akin to God saying, "Yes sir, you've picked the right spot to make your beer." At the nearly unheard-of depth of only 55 feet, they hit their gusher. And it flowed strong and pure and kept on flowing.

But being the never-satisfied Czechs and Germans that they were, they didn't stop there. They kept drilling deeper, nonetheless, just to make sure. Still, the water flowed and it flows still.

This is important, of course, since water is the first and most important ingredient of beer. In the case of Shiner, its purity and quality is in bigger hands than those of mere men. The well they first dug at the little brewery was not just a success, or a buzzword; it was a sign. Moreover, it was one that was appreciated and understood, becoming the centerpiece and main ingredient of the glorious elixir of which you now drink.

For their part, the Czechs and the Germans who dug said well just made sure the end-product didn't taste like water.

For them, the "artesians," and—yes—even the Carthusian monks, we can all be thankful.

A cold Shiner Bock shot in The Cedar Door in Austin, Texas.

CH3

WHEN LIFE HANDS YOU A LEMON

MAKE LEMONADE

(OR MAYBE SOMETHING A LITTLE STRONGER)

     **1919 – 1940**

In Texas, we've the annoying habit (one man's opinion, anyway) of naming lakes, dams, freeways and pretty much anything that requires large amounts of concrete, taxpayer money and other people's property, after politicians. The delicious irony of such a tradition seems lost on the honorees themselves, as Austin and the D. of C. remain full of pork procurers whose hearts go all aflutter at the thought of having 50 or 60,000 acres or so confiscated, flooded and named in their honor.

Formerly when this occurred, said politicians generally at least had the decency to be dead, but of late, having "late" in front of your name seems no longer a requirement for becoming a landmark.

George Bush, the father, and utterer of the infamous "read my lips, 'no new taxes,'" pledge has had (delicious irony rears its fair head yet again) toll roads named after him for years around here. Even Lyndon Johnson, the jowly and profane man from Stonewall, under whose watch America suffered its greatest identity crisis, he, too, has more than his share of modern-day pyramids. In the late '60s, he was immortalized—appropriately enough—via a superhighway that doesn't really go anywhere—the I-635 loop around Dallas. It's also the one most likely to get you killed.

Continuing this theme of "truth in advertising re: public monuments," old U.S. Senator Morris Sheppard got his less-than-household name slapped on a dam. The Morris Sheppard Dam that flooded the canyons along the Brazos River in Palo Pinto County is nowhere near the biggest impoundment that ever bore his name, though. The honorable Mr. Sheppard, you see, is the Texan who introduced the successful Senate resolution for the 18th Amendment establishing national prohibition and thereby cutting off all flow of beer, wine and liquor. His resolution passed on a wave of national temperance and—yes, owing to World War I—some anti-German sentiment. So it was that Prohibition went into effect in Texas in 1918, just three years after Kosmos Spoetzl had taken over the brewery.

Senator Sheppard's dam, when they finished it, inundated a town called Pickwick and wiped it off the face of the map forever. A betting man of the day (though this amusement,

too, was under siege) probably would've wagered a fair amount that Shiner would meet its end very soon as well, and no less gruesomely.

They wouldn't have been accounting for the chubby German man, though.

Morris Sheppard is oft quoted as having said, "There is as much chance of repealing the eighteenth amendment as there is for a hummingbird to fly to the planet Mars with the Washington Monument tied to its tail."

Kosmos Spoetzl, never prone to such grand pronouncements, ended up with a building named after him, as well, thank you very much. It was his building, though, not confiscated from the sweat of someone else's brow.

And nowadays, on blue, cliff-lined waters a hundred feet or so over the remains of Pickwick, boats of all kinds tow skiers and haul fishermen—most oblivious to the fact the dam on Possum Kingdom Lake is named after one Morris Sheppard. Most have probably never even heard of him.

They've heard of Kosmos Spoetzl, though. They know about *his* monument. Chances are, they've got a couple six packs of said monument in their ice chest.

I guess hummingbirds are stronger than we give 'em credit for. So too, apparently, are health-challenged Bavarians.

In spite of the best efforts of politicians looking to save us from ourselves, Shiner never went the way of Pickwick, though not without some considerable effort.

Back in the early years of Kosmos' reign at the Home Brewery, national leaders on the other side of the Atlantic were fighting not the evils of drink, but one another. Several years before, on April 6, 1917, the United States had declared war on

Germany, joining the fray that had been ongoing since 1914. With that done, the march towards prohibition picked up its pace even more under the guise of "the war effort."

That German immigrants were at the forefront of a lot of brewing in the United States probably didn't help their cause. Whether spoken or not—and it was spoken a whole lot more back then—distrust of Germans and German descendants was palpable.

For their part, the residents of Shiner went out of their way to make certain everyone knew that while they may have been German by birth or heritage, they were American by choice. Parades, with lots of flags, bunting and Uncle Sam impersonators became a regular fixture on the local social calendar as the war went on. No small number of the town's young men joined the service and were soon shipped into the fray, several being killed or wounded in action.

One would think the shedding of blood, whether that blood was descended from Germany or not, would quiet the questioners. Probably not, though. Doubtless, there were still catcalls and nasty comments directed the way of many a Shinerite during this time, yet they'd survived too much to come all this way and be bowed by a bit of ignorance and hate. And certainly Shiner, being more homogenous in terms of its population of immigrants and children of immigrants, could circle its wagons in the face of ugliness and gather strength from neighbors and family.

"The Great War" ended in November of 1918, and the celebration began with the ringing of the church bells and sounding of sirens at five o'clock in the morning, when the news came in from across the Atlantic.

But thanks to Senator Sheppard and compatriots, the celebration would be limited to bell ringing and "near beer" for the boys returning from war. The town of Shiner had held one "last feast before the town goes dry" on June 27 of that year to mark the last time beer could be legally had before enforcement of Prohibition in Texas. By the time the veterans of the war made it back home, even Shiner was bone-dry.

Or was it?

This, of course, is the spot at which a wink and nudge should be inserted into this tale. There are, of course, press releases, and then there is always the real story. For press release purposes, the Home Brewery sought to make its way through the obstacle laid in front of it by producing a brew that contained less than 0.5 percent alcohol—much akin to the "non-alcoholic" beers you can find on the store shelves nowadays (where they generally stay for an extended period of time). Kosmos also used a good part of the brewery to make ice. Saloons in town became respectable "restaurants" and, all in all, people around town just shrugged their shoulders at the folly of "the great experiment" and probably said a coarse word or two about being the guinea pigs in such an undertaking. Otherwise, they went on with life.

And everybody in Texas drives 65 on the Interstate, too. Otherwise, we might run over the Easter Bunny or the Tooth Fairy on the way to check on our longhorns and oil wells.

The old ones around town—the ones who were little kids during those days—will tell you without hesitation they never stopped making beer down at the brewery. They remember a ride in Daddy's truck through town, with a stop by the loading dock to "get some ice." There was always that extra box or two that got loaded into the truck along with the ice.

"So-and-so knew old what's-his-face, who knew that if you went by the dock at a certain time, they'd be able to get you that 'package' you'd been wanting. Just tell 'em so-and-so sent you."

For every press release, there's a half-dozen or so "off-the-records" or "unidentified sources."

Law-breaking? That's a dicey one to put a hard and fast answer on from this far down the road. Remember, if you will, what Kosmos and a goodly number of his neighbors had been through in their journeys to Texas. By the letter of the law, yeah, you could make a case against them if you'd a mind to. But people sometimes do what they have to do when survival is in question, and this was exactly the case as the teens turned

---

The old ones around town—the ones who were little kids during those days—will tell you without hesitation they never stopped making beer down at the brewery.

---

into the '20s and a once-promising young business turned into a white elephant made of barley and hops.

There is a rumor—most likely nothing more than that, but colorful, nonetheless...the story was that, occasionally, Kosmos would send a shipment of beer to Houston. On one of those trips, the driver of the truck made a wrong turn and ended up going the wrong way down a one-way street. Pulled over by the law, the back was opened up and the illicit cargo discovered. As the legend goes, Kosmos, who could have left his driver hanging out to dry, stepped forward and faced the music, being sent to Leavenworth for 18 months. Supposedly, just before being released from jail, Kosmos had his shoes stolen and left the place without any.

Most likely, this is one of those stories only partially or maybe not at all true, but one that's taken on its own life over the years and one not at all out of character with times that caused people to either quit or use their imaginations.

Beer, as it turned out, had not been the evil some had portrayed it to be. Endless lines of innocent people being thrown into cattle cars and shipped to their deaths at the whim of insane fist-shakers showed us without doubt there were far darker shadows than any cast by barley, malt and hops.

The majority of the time, imagination served the brewery far better than it did the errant Houston truck driver. A system was supposedly developed whereby whenever a federal agent or "revenooer" was making his way towards Shiner for an inspection (generally by train), friendly eyes up the tracks would sound the alarm by placing a call to the brewery with plenty of time to ensure things were in order. Before the agent would get to town, Boggy Creek, which runs adjacent to the brewhouse, would suddenly become awash with white foam.

Environmentally unsound as this may have been, it did manage to help the brewery pass inspection and live to make "ice" and "near beer" another day. The warning given from the next town also served to ensure that the friendly soul on the other end of the phone line would continue to receive his supply of contraband as well.

Even the fishermen along parts of the itinerant creek prospered, as the relaxed and suddenly more carefree fish were always easier to catch during "Revenooer Rises."

One longtime driver for the brewery, Calvin Cosmo "Cracker" Wallace (whom you'll read more about later) remembers the story of a different revenooer by the name of Wheeler, who would always call ahead to let Kosmos know he was coming because he wanted to be certain there would be real beer for him to enjoy when he arrived. The wink-and-nudge way of doing business applied, apparently, as much to the government as it did to the people who "didn't" make beer any more.

Kosmos, for his part, remained as cheery and upbeat as ever,

still handing out his shiny nickels to the kids (though maybe less often) and, most likely, offering a discreet wink to those who might inquire of where a man could take care of a man's thirst.

There are press releases, and then there's reality.

Reality, indeed. In 1921, in a raw reminder that trouble seems to always come in groups, came and roosted once again on the metal roof of the already-beleaguered brewery. Elsa, Kosmos' wife, died of cancer. Not much has been said of her in this tale and this is simply because not a great deal is known. She did not cut nearly as wide a swath through life as her husband did. At least not on this side of the Atlantic. Certainly she did not have the kind of presence her husband maintained around town. But this was a different age. Having come from the Old World and accompanied her man through his sojourn in search of a place more gentle to his health, she clung to the notion—more widely held then—that she was to remain in the background while he did what needed to be done. Wherever that took them.

They had met in Cairo while Kosmos worked at the Pyramid Brewery. She had served as a domestic for German expatriates. Kosmos' first wife, and mother to daughter Cecile, had died years earlier in Germany. Cecile, nearly grown, had remained in Germany when Kosmos left for Cairo.

Shortly after Elsa's death, Kosmos returned to Germany and brought Cecile ("Miss Celie," as she would later become known) back to Shiner. Taking over many office duties and maintaining Kosmos' home life, she quickly became a fixture both around the brewery and in town.

Elsewhere, the 1920s roared. Mainly they did their roaring in the big cities of the North and Northeast and in the movies Hollywood turned out one after another. At the brewery, they more or less limped along.

"I got nothing but truuuble and debts," Kosmos was known to say in his broken English on more than one occasion during the rough times. Even then, he was prone to laugh shortly after saying it and getting on with business.

Miss Celie did her best to pick up the language and became quite adept at growing a garden, milking cows, making butter and generally taking care of the menagerie of animals that roamed the grounds of the brewery. Along with the sheep, there were deer, peacocks and the odd goat here and there.

"There was one Christmas during the Prohibition where we had two dollars in the account for the brewery and 75 cents in the house," Miss Celie remembered.

"We owed the boys another $10 each, but we just gave them what we could. They stuck with us, though, because we were like family. We'd still had a Christmas party with the kids and the babies and all. We were one big family."

With the double whammy of Prohibition and the Depression after 1929, everyone continued to hope that the next year would be the last year of "the great experiment."

Prior to 1918, there had been over 6,600 breweries—many small like Kosmos'. By 1933, when repeal finally came about, very few remained. Even larger brewers like the Anheuser Busch brewery in San Antonio became casualties of the long dry spell. And whether totally by the book or not, The Spoetzl Brewery was defiantly one of the few that remained standing, staggered though it was.

Finally, on September 15, 1933, beer could again be sold in Shiner. With decent advance notice, Kosmos, Celie and "the boys" worked feverishly to make certain that at the stroke of midnight, they would be ready for the thirsty masses. "Texas Export" was the new brew they introduced that night, courtesy of new brewmaster August Haslbeck, a nephew of Kosmos who'd joined the brewery in 1930 and served as brewmaster from 1934 to 1966. The long night was over and Kosmos was far from the only one smiling.

Though the Depression still hung on, at least now there was beer. And for the little brewery, that meant there was at least a chance. Kosmos began thinking of ways to expand and improve the brewery. Many of the additions to the place came from the remains of the scores of breweries that fell victim to Prohibition. Without much money, he'd go to old, defunct breweries and buy equipment at extremely reduced prices and cobble it into the workings of the Spoetzl Brewery. Nothing fancy, but it worked.

The same could not be said for the world at large. Europe was hurtling towards another war, more ugly even than the one before. There would again be anti-German sentiment to be endured, but endurance had already proven itself to be in plentiful supply, given the years just passed. Twenty-seven employees were now working full-time at the brewery, and the old distribution network throughout Central Texas was being rebuilt and improved upon, reaching even, for the first time (legally, anyway), to Houston.

By the early '40s, a new bottling room was added to the old tin building that still survived from 1909 and the name (though not the formula) of "Texas Export" was changed to "Texas Special Beer."

Debts that had been incurred over the lean years were slowly shrinking, and Kosmos' plans for the place, which had languished in his head for the last 15 years or so, might

finally now see the light of day.

Only water would now flow in Boggy Creek—barring accidents, of course. The fish would go back to that cheerless life their human counterparts had been made to endure for all those years.

Beer, as it turned out, had not been the evil some had portrayed it to be. Endless lines of innocent people being thrown into cattle cars and shipped to their deaths at the whim of insane fist-shakers showed us without doubt there were far darker shadows than any cast by barley, malt and hops.

Those "dry" fifteen years from 1918 to 1933 hadn't really dried up anything. Certainly not the longing for a beer, nor even more certainly the ingenuity of those willing to slake such a thirst. The prohibitionists had had their day and were left with not much to show for it, save a fair amount of violence and millions, if not billions, of dollars lost to an enervated underworld. The social high horse is never an easy pony to ride and often takes its rider places never intended.

Bitterness, certainly, would have been an understandable refuge for the few independent brewers like Kosmos Spoetzl, who managed to survive the whole mess. Then again, that's a crop that never grew well around Shiner.

There are species that do thrive in this part of the world, though. Those that can be most counted on—when faced with prolonged drought—simply extend their roots more deeply into the soil.

Sometimes, even those transplanted from far away.

ABOVE: Boggy Creek would never be the same: Kosmos and friends toast the end of "the great experiment."

PROHI
ENDS A

BITION
T LAST!

LEFT & RIGHT: To say there was joy in Shiner at the end of Prohibition would be more than a mild understatement. Finally, you could get something other than a Root Beer Float.

"The Pride of Texas"

SHINER

TEXAS

SPOETZL BRE

BEER
EXPORT

★ SHINER

SHINER
TEXAS

WERY

K.SPOETZL / HASLBECK

SMALLEST COMMERCIAL BREW KETTLE IN AMERICA

LEFT: It's nice to be the man: Kosmos at the helm, in the office.

RIGHT: Kosmos and Mr. Haslbeck do a bit of quality control. Watch that cigar, Kosmos.

el Brewery

NER TEXAS

DODGE

CHAPTER

FATHER! LOOKAHERE!

1940-1950

Those initials, (the ones on the current brewery building) "K. Spoetzl Brewery," the Alamo Iron Works in San Antone--where Father all those years bought those little things he needed, you know- they donated those to him. And when the bricklayer, Mr. Sontagg, and Son, shows up and they put them up, it was a Tuesday in November and the weather was drizzling outside and all the windows were sweating. And I went outside and saw Mr. Sontagg and I said, "Mr. Sontagg, how far along are you?" And Mr. Sontagg said, "You get back in that office, you make us all nervous here. But your father is coming any minute."

About 10 minutes or 15 minutes later, I saw Father coming with his Ford Coupe. He always had a Ford Coupe, and he stopped here on the driveway. And when I run across the street to the driveway by Father—he always wore a waistcoat and suspenders—and he had his hands in there, and he looked up there. And I said, "Father, lookahere: 'K. Spoetzl Brewery,' isn't it pretty?" And when I came close to Father, I saw tears in his eyes.

He said, "Yes, Celie, it is pretty."

He looked a little longer. I didn't say nothing.

He turned around and went to the house. And I went back to the office.

I don't know what went through my Father's mind. All those years, from 1915 to 1948, without any credit rating, you know, that's a hard time. And being a stranger, and he don't manage the English language so good, but he made it.

Many people I knew, they say, "That Mr. Spoetzl down there, he works so hard. He never gonna make it with his little brewery."

There it is.

He made it.

Yep.

From an interview with Ms. Celie, aged 82. Recorded in 1976.

I
n that recording, Miss Celie's voice remained thickly accented with the sound of the old country, despite more than a half a century of sometimes-uncertain living in Texas. And even though she was less than a year from the end of her own life, the voice was strong, with the occasional crack, here and there. Sometimes she'd break into a wheeze of laughter at some silly little thing remembered. Sometimes, a long pause and a hard swallow, probably thinking about things and people and times that won't be coming back.

The voice was overall strong, though. The memory, clear with detail that mere writers of books can never recreate nearly as well as the ones who were actually there. Miss Celie didn't just know the man, she was *of* the man. The last remainder of himself that he would leave behind to this world—that—and the beer, of course. And his little brewery.

And as of that drizzly day in November 1947, when windows sweated and an old German man cried, the little brewery with Kosmos Spoetzl's cigar-stained fingerprints all over it—once and for all—had his name on it for everyone to see.

Mr. Sontagg and Son did a fine job of making it so, despite the rain and cold and any nervousness they felt from Miss Celie looking over their shoulders. The work got done in time, and Kosmos knew nothing about it 'til Miss Celie called his attention to it.

It's the same sign you see when you walk up to the place. If ever you have the occasion to make your way into the Hospitality Room, stop for a minute and "lookahere."

The old man never would've put the sign up himself. He was too busy with other stuff. He'd finally, in the '40's, gotten a little more flush with the world and had the opportunity to put some money back in the place. The old brick building you know so well from the photos is the one he built starting in the mid-'40s. Brick had permanence with which the old corrugated metal brewhouse could never compete. But even then, the bricks were salvaged from somewhere or another. Permanence, yes, but extravagance...well, that just wasn't his way.

He'd told people more than once when the building was completed, he could rest a little bit easier. Not that he ever really did. Maybe it was his soul he was talking about that would do the resting even if his body was less than accepting of such things.

It was his baby. He'd nursed it, taught it how to walk, bandaged its bloodied knees, and now—just maybe—he could see it living beyond his own allotment of years.

Others had witnessed his work; being moved enough by it to acknowledge it with something permanent. And so it was that the plot to put the sign up was hatched. But for all the durability of the iron letters that went up on the brick, "K. Spoetzl" is etched even more indelibly in the memories of a few whose hearts go on beating.

This world lost its hold on Miss Celie in June of '77 and with her went about the closest approximation we had to what Kosmos must've sounded like.

There was "Cracker," though. He could still do a pretty fair approximation of the broken English and string of German cuss-words one might've heard when K. Spoetzl "went to fussin' at you."

Truth be told, the brewery wasn't the first to get Kosmos' name (although it was spelled differently). Calvin Cosmo Wallace had it even before that. Most everybody has always called him Cracker, though. Cracker's daddy worked nights in the engine room of the old place for 59 years. His Uncle Joe worked there for 63. So pretty much from the time he was born, in 1938, Cracker was around the brewery and more specifically, running around with Kosmos.

Calvin became "Cracker," given that's what he always seemed to have in his mouth or close by as a little kid.

"Boy, you keep eating those, you gonna turn into a cracker," Kosmos had told him more than once. Eventually, it stuck. The little black kid stuck to Kosmos, too.

Here, a little bit of historical perspective is most likely in order. Texas in the 1940s was, like much of the country, very

much segregated. The deeply rooted nature of it, however, wasn't a part of the immigrants' experience. Certainly, many of them had been at the blunt end of it themselves on more than one occasion. But for Kosmos, that was other people's ugliness. On the other hand, his mentorship of young Cracker wasn't a matter of making a statement against something he viewed as wrong; it was simply about treating people the way he'd want to be treated.

The brewery Cracker hung around—can't you just hear the modern-day Nannies registering their disapproval?—was growing. People throughout Central Texas were buying the beer and the trucks were kept busy day and night getting it to where the thirsts were. Kosmos still did his runs around the country with a Number 3 washtub of iced- down beer in the back and, much of the time, Cracker, along with Kosmos' part-collie dog.

Be it in his old Ford or on the grounds of the brewery, wherever Kosmos was found, so too were animals in numbers worthy of Noah. As widely repeated throughout the town and reported even in the *Shiner Gazette*, his love for animals was very nearly the end of him on at least one occasion. A 12-point buck deer named Billy, for some years, roamed the property with impunity. And just as the sheep were a convenient way to keep the grass mowed and fertilized, Billy did his part to keep things looking nice by gladly eating Kosmos' cigar butts whenever offered. On this particular day, Kosmos stood out in the pasture across from the brewery feeding Billy a fresh batch of his nicotine-laced delicacies. Having run through the lot, Kosmos turned to head back in. Billy would have none of it, however. He wanted more, and registered his displeasure by attacking his master, nearly goring him at least once or twice, before running off and madly jumping the fence, a string of German cuss-words following him across Boggy Creek as he

continued on towards town and some madly-imagined goal. The cigar store, maybe?

Kosmos, straightening his clothes, now even more rumpled than usual, headed for the Ford and gave chase without success. After terrorizing the town—if indeed a cigar-butt-crazed deer can do such a thing—a local cowboy managed to lasso the fugitive, whereupon he was promptly extradited back to the brewery and barbecued that weekend.

Old-time justice in Texas was nothing if not swift and—quite often—creative.

The Spoetzl affection for animals was not limited to just Kosmos. Miss Celie, though a confirmed city girl living in Hamburg in her previous life, began each day by milking the numerous cows kept on the property, and fed the chickens, peacocks and whatever else needed feeding. One suspects cigar butts were not a part of her fare, though this is only speculation.

On a typical day, this routine was followed by a full day in the brewery office, managing the books: payroll, vendors, customers and whatever else might crop up. As the '40s waned and the new buildings were completed, she got more and more comfortable with the daily workings of the operation.

But not long after Kosmos' name went up on the side of the new building, his health began to fail. Longstanding heart problems were beginning to catch up with him. On June 17, 1950, he died.

The viewing was at the house on the brewery grounds. Cracker, who was 12 at the time, went to the house and stayed on the porch for two days, not wanting to leave the old man's side. He refused to go to any of his family's gatherings until they laid Kosmos to rest. For many of the years since then, a visit to Kosmos' grave during the holiday season would reveal a carefully placed Christmas tree, always the work of Cracker.

Fence posts, however, would never be festive again.

Of course, on that day in the middle of June of 1950, Kosmos had just arrived at a place we're all headed to eventually. And while we try not to think about it much, in the back

FAR LEFT: Everybody liked it when Kosmos came around.

LEFT: Nearing the end of a long road: Kosmos, near the sign Miss Celie put up for him in the late 1940s.

ABOVE: A couple of young bucks: Kosmos and Billy.

of our minds, and sometimes in the things we do each day, we strive to create something bigger and, hopefully, less perishable than our own frail bodies. It has been said that the definition of faith is planting trees even when you know full well that you'll not be around to enjoy their shade. Surely the man had that. Faith, fearlessness, *cojones*, whatever you choose to call it, he had a full measure of it and applied it liberally to survive those days of two dollars in the bank account, prohibitionist zealots and more than a couple of Don Quixote-like expeditions that seemed to lead nowhere.

...beers raised in toast, and laughs from stories true and not, because this was Kosmos, after all.

Some of a provincial nature might well say that where he ended up was right smack-dab in the *middle* of nowhere. Maybe this is so. But from all indications, this is precisely where he was supposed to be all along. Convincing cases can be made both for and against the existence of fate and predetermination. But surely Kosmos Spoetzl's life is as good an argument as one could find for the affirmative argument.

The middle of nowhere? Sure. But it's the people who know how to take "nowhere" and turn it into somewhere that end up carving out the biggest pieces of real estate in our hearts. In this regard, Kosmos owned more acreage than the King Ranch. Certainly a bunch of hearts had been moved by this old German's laugh and smile because on June 19th at the cemetery, there were faces of all colors with little in common outside the tears that ran down them. And there were lumps in throats about broken English that would be heard no longer and old washtubs in the back of an old car that would now be empty.

But there was gladness, too, and yes, beers raised in toast, and laughs from stories true and not, because this was Kosmos, after all. And he would have simply said of his passing that he was tired and worn-out, and since everything was paid for, this was as good a time as any to call it a life.

Tears still fell, though. Appropriately enough, into glasses of the thing he loved most.

Some of the greatest regrets we end up dragging around in this life are those that stem from losing loved ones with whom maybe we haven't fully shown our love. As at every such occasion, there were surely people filing by the casket at

Kosmos Spoetzl's funeral who'd wished they'd told him how much he meant to them.

That old sign that Miss Celie, along with the iron works and the bricklayers, had put on his beloved little brewery, was their way of doing just that.

Certainly, Kosmos, for his part, left no doubt about his feelings toward us.

BAVARIAN STYLE

TASTE/SMILE

LEFT: Calvin Cosmo Wallace, also known as "Cracker" to Mr. Spoetzl, circa 1950.

ABOVE: Kosmos enjoying the fruits of his labor, circa 1950.

BLUE CHRISTMAS: The old man may not have been around for Christmas anymore, but that didn't stop Cracker from taking Christmas to the old man.

"...I do not know where time goes and when he said the other day that it was twenny five years since you all went out to Texas and I began to cry, dear sister, because I do not believe that we are like to see each other any more."

FROM A "LETTER TO A TEXAS IMMIGRANT" IN JOHN GRAVES' *GOODBYE TO A RIVER*

CHAPTER 5

A WOMAN'S PLACE

★ ★★ ★★ IS IN THE ★ ★★ ★

BREWHOUSE

1950-1966

Cosmopolitan magazine, had it existed in 1950 (and I don't know whether it did or it didn't, and if it did, it certainly wasn't what it is now) would have done well for itself to visit Shiner. There it would have found not much that was "cosmopolitan" but if it'd made its way down to 603 East Brewery Street, it'd have encountered the only female brewery proprietress in the country.

Of course, she wouldn't have been brash, outlandish, or vocal enough for its taste, most likely. In fact, she continued to engage in totally un-cool activities such as the daily feeding of the chickens, peacocks and innumerable brewery grounds creatures, plus the milking of cows, in addition to making sure the beer kept flowing in a manner suitable to Kosmos' wishes.

The methods of discernment employed by our culture are odd—if not downright twisted—when it comes to deciding who is worthy of press and the adulation it brings. This being the 1950s, though, "respectable" women did not infringe on the world of the man—especially not that most brutish of places— a brewery. Yes, there had been "Rosie the Riveter" and the like building airplanes during World War II, but Miss Celie's newfound and not necessarily welcomed position of propri- etress of the K. Spoetzl Brewery was unheard-of. Never mind that she didn't really want it and had certainly left no trail of stabbed backs on her way to the top; women just didn't belong in certain places.

Even in a negative way, it didn't draw attention that in the little town of Shiner, Texas, there was a lady running the whole show. Certainly, Miss Celie was not one to call attention to herself. A widow, with one daughter, who herself was widowed, Miss Celie was much like the reluctant King Saul of the Old Testament when she became the nation's sole female brewery president when it seemed that was the only thing that could be done.

Gus Haslbeck, a relative of Kosmos', had gone to brewmas- ter's school in the old country and taken over those duties in the '30s, so at least those technical matters were in hands other than Celie's. Her lot had been the office and the bookkeeping since her arrival, and this she would continue much as before.

The unstated job that lay in front of her was ensuring her father's wishes for the place would be followed and, when necessary, expanded or built upon. That would be the tricky part. But given the large number of first-person witnesses to Kosmos' way of doing things, it wasn't as though Miss Celie would have to do much education in that regard. The more immediate matter, of course, was the gaping wound left by the absence of such a huge figure as the old man. Though this, being a shared hurt, was gradually worked through as such losses almost always are.

Certainly he'd have never wanted the clinking of the bottles to stop serenading the town just because his watch had come to an end. Everyone knew that fact and carried on as such. As Cracker had said on more than one occasion, the last thing you wanted was "for Kosmos to go to fussin' at you." It was certainly not a singular opinion around the brewery, and just the echo of a broken-English tirade ringing in everyone's heads was more than enough to maintain their focus on keeping things right.

And you know...it is at precisely such a point as this that many a business has gone to its end. A visionary passes on and soon, too, so does the vision. This is precisely why, in retro- spect, it was so important that Miss Celie was there when she was and, further, that she was willing, against previous plans and perhaps better judgment, to take on the role of caretaker and insurer that the vision would go on.

With all the debts paid off, she could have sold right then and there, collected a nice sum of money and returned to Germany, as had been her notion all along. Not a soul around Shiner would have blamed her if she had. But she took seriously her promises and maybe—just maybe—saw that there was something here that needed tending to in hope of a future nobody else could quite yet see.

The thing about institutions that stand the test of time, let alone all the other infirmities of human endeavor, is that,

generally, there is someone—or several someones—who sees, the glint of fruition long before anyone else. Kosmos certainly saw much that made others shake their heads in wonder at his stick-to-itiveness, and by way of blood, Miss Celie, over time, contracted the same infection.

So, as the fifties rolled on at 603 E. Brewery Street, near the intersection of Improbable Street and Unlikely Road, the little brewery continued its journey to the time when people would plan road trips and whole vacations around the goal of merely saying they'd been there. Growth was not incredible, but steady and reasonable. Bigness, of course, had never been the goal anyway. History, even in 1950, had already shown largeness as a near-surefire way to blandness.

In terms of "events," the remainder of the fifties and early sixties were devoid of many milestones that would elicit much ink in a history book more disciplined than this one; but then, that may well be the beauty of what Miss Celie did in her time at the helm of a ship she never meant to steer. Longnecks continued the clink of their merry German music on the bottling line, men still went to work every day, knowing they could come back the next day, and the country's only female brewery owner and president stayed pleasantly out of any popular culture spotlight, such as it was at the time. It wasn't, "Look at me, I'm doing something unheard-of up to now." It was, "Father didn't want us to become too big for our britches, and there are plenty of 'big brewers' out there, we just want to be 'honest brewers,' true to ourselves and the people who drink our beer."

Such sentiments didn't bring *Cosmopolitan* or any such magazine of the day calling, but they did ensure the continued loyalty of the locals and even the occasional piece of press from the big city—even if said big city wasn't New York.

In 1953, columnist Sig Byrd of the *Houston Chronicle*, came to town—originally to write an article about the Kaspar Wire Works across the road from the brewery.

...The Spoetzl Brewery, a charming Old-World kind of place, is still the smallest brewery in Big Texas, while the Kaspar Wire Works is the world's largest manufacturer of gymnasium locker room baskets.

Kosmos Spoetzl died in 1950, leaving the brewery, which stands on the bank of Boggy Creek, looking like a miniature castle on the Rhine, to his daughter, Cecile. Gus Kaspar is still living, but has turned the management of the wire works over to his son, Arthur, and his grandson, Dan.

Calling on Arthur and Dan the other day, I found them supervising a tool-up job for the production of a new wire product. It looks like a folding egg-beater, but it's a taco fryer, for cooking tacos.

Arthur gave me one of the fryers, which I believe is the first taco fryer in Houston. Since we don't fry tacos at our house, I will be happy to present this to the first reader, not a Chronicle *employee, calling for it in person. If I'm not in my office, you'll find it lying on my desk. Just take it along and leave your name, address and phone number.*

Miss Celie gave me a case of Shiner Beer. I am not giving any of that away.

Shiner is a charming town, mostly because of the Spoetzl Brewery, which is protected by Saint Gambrinus, the patron of beer drinkers, and is a delightful place to visit, as you shall see in a later report.

That last little bit there, where Mr. Byrd mentions "Saint Gambrinus", is either modern-day prophecy or, at the very least, one heckuva piece of foreshadowing, given the fact he wrote that article in 1953. Thirty-six years after this was written, when the brewery came very near to closing its doors, a man from San Antonio by the name of Carlos Alvarez (like Kosmos, an immigrant living in San Antonio) would purchase the troubled operation and finance the success it enjoys today. The name of Mr. Alvarez's company? Gambrinus.

You can't make this kind of stuff up.

But we've got miles to go and lots of beer to drink before we get to that part of the story...

Miss Celie saw her role as a custodian of her father's dream. To her, that dream was about the beer, not slick marketing gimmicks the big brands took to their heights in the '50s and '60s. So while Budweiser did national jingles and grocery store promotions with Ed McMahon encouraging us to "Pick-a-Pair of Six Packs" (no 12-packs in those days), Shiner's marketing was carried out on a far more personal level. "Road men" loaded up their cars with matches, ashtrays, coasters, lighted signs, tap handles and whatever other kind of gee-gaw they could find and each day hit all the bars in their territory. As part of their duties, they were expected to sit down for a while and have a beer or two with the bar proprietor, maybe offer up a round for the customers, and then it was on to the next place down the road.

The endless glad-handing of life as a roadman was not a calling for the anti-social nor those unable to hold their beer.

LEFT: Miss Celie with her spiffy crew.

Most likely, one of the favorite phrases of Kosmos during his time at the helm of the place echoed through their heads as they did their 12-ounce waltzes throughout the little towns of Central Texas—"Drink all zee beer you vant, boys," the old man had said. "Just don't get yourselv drunk." A nice sentiment in theory, no doubt, but more difficult to execute—especially considering that the last thing you wanted as a road man was for anybody to see you not finishing the very beer you're trying to convince them is the best thing this side of the Pearly Gates.

Yoakum, Hallettsville, Hocheim, Weimar, everywhere there was a domino room, pool table or juke box, Shiner's road warriors made their rounds bearing gifts of calendars, matchbooks, neon signs, clocks and a couple of good jokes. On the outside, they'd make it as far as places like Austin, Corpus Christi and Houston, but in those days, those were the very edges of the earth—at least in the Shiner world.

She did, in '58, introduce non-returnable bottles—something that sounds strange now, but at the time most longneck bottles, like old soda pop bottles, were returned, washed and re-used. Nobody back then talked about being "green" or "renewable resources," but for years that's just what most brewers were—at least until the expense of it became too hard to justify. And with all the big boys out there going to the disposables, so too, did Miss Celie.

In '64, she brought in her daughter, Rosa Leach, to help run the office and thus introduced the third generation of the family to the business. But probably the biggest thing Miss Celie did during her run at the helm was to hire John Hybner in February of 1966. Within a few years, he would become brewmaster and remain in that position until June 1, 2005.

Miss Celie, however, after nearly 16 years of doing what no other woman in the country had done for even one year, was

Miss Celie saw her role as a custodian of her father's dream. To her, that dream was about the beer, not slick marketing gimmicks the big brands took to their heights in the 50's and 60's.

Given the way things are these days, such operations are looked back upon with mouths aghast, but remember too that this was a time that distances between Texas towns were often measured not by miles but six-packs. This is not to say it was a good thing, but it was the way of the time, for better or worse. "Pacing," the grizzled veterans of the circuit would offer up as their secret to survival. But that's a strategy that doesn't mix well with the current vogue of "zero tolerance." Most likely it's a good thing business isn't done that way anymore, but there are still some of us who would mourn just a little the passing of another personal way of doing business that's now gone the way of wooden kegs and returnable bottles.

Miss Celie on her watch allowed the old ways to remain beyond the time when others had disposed of them and moved onto the slicker methods. Not out of any philosophical hard line, but just because she thought these were the things her father would have been loath to dispose of. The discarded machinery of other breweries had often been his only method of keeping the place running and profitable. Miss Celie simply continued to follow his methods. In retrospect, maybe she did so longer than prudent, but without a doubt it was always with the desire to honor him and his little brewery.

growing weary of the weight of keeping her father's beloved brewery open and profitable, while doing so in a manner of which he'd approve. Her inner turmoil about how best to ensure the future of the place had preceded the celebration in 1965 of 50 years of family ownership. Beyond the celebration, the 50th anniversary had caused her to pause and consider what would happen after her passing. Within a couple of years of arriving at the brewery, it became clear her daughter Rosa had no interest in taking over. Even her work in the office was short-lived and thus made it clear to Miss Celie that if the brewery were to continue, it would have to be outside family hands. Gus Haslbeck, one of Kosmos' nephews, was at the time serving as brewmaster as he had since the '30's but he was getting on in years and could offer no long-term solution.

Would-be suitors to the place had come through on occasion, but she'd always rebuffed their advances. She especially didn't like the thought of someone coming in, buying the place, spending a little money on it and just turning around and selling again. If she were to sell to someone other than family, she would need to feel like there would be stability.

When Bill Bigler had shown up expressing an interest in the place, that's exactly what he promised. A former brewmaster at Lone Star in San Antonio, he'd wanted to try his own hand at running the whole show and convinced Miss Celie he would love Kosmos' beloved place as his own and see it through the next era, whatever that might bring.

In 1966, Miss Celie announced to a gathering of the brewery employees that she had come to the agonizing decision to sell. Bill Bigler was introduced, and on July 1st the brewery officially changed hands. She tried to assure everyone that things would continue as they had before and that all this change was for the best. But like someone who owns what was once a small puppy that can no longer be taken care of and has to be given to others, there is always the mixture of guilt, trepidation and hope.

The brewery had changed hands but Miss Celie remained in the little white house across the way, hoping that the "K. Spoetzl Brewery" sign up above the door that had moved the old man to tears 20 years before would remain. She may have relinquished her monetary interest in the brewery, but the interest in her heart was not for sale. And so she stayed...watching.

Miss Celie had only intended to be in Shiner for five years or so when Kosmos convinced her to come with him in 1922. She would do her best to honor her father, help him set his business in order, and return to her city life in Hamburg and the family that'd told her not to go in the first place.

"Celie," they'd said, "Why do you want to go to this place where it's so hot and so far away?"

She had no good answer, outside of the fact it was her father. She'd go to Texas and come back as soon as possible.

Fifty-four years later in that same little house, she sat down for a tape-recorded interview and told the story of the day she sold the brewery. The memory of it all, right down to the specific times of day of each event, remained vivid in her mind. Though she was 82 years old at the time, she could tell you everything.

Everything except the story of her return to Germany. She would've had to make that one up. Never happened.

And there was, as in any life, regret. One in particular that stood above all others. After only two years, Mr. Bigler sold the place again. To him, it was business and you can't fault a man for doing what he thinks prudent, but to Miss Celie, this wasn't a building full of machinery, it was "Father." His hands had touched every inch of that brewhouse and all that was in it and had, in fact, cobbled most of it together from damned near scratch. To Miss Celie, that building was not the sum of its parts, but like our physical being, the container of something

that can't be seen or bought or sold or felt. Yes, there were souls in that place, "Father's" and everybody else's who'd ever been hired, fired, loved, cussed and cared for by the old man.

There's no column on a ledger sheet for soul, though. None of us can see it and there's one helluva lot of people in this world who seem incapable of even feeling it. That the person to whom she had sold the brewery couldn't "feel" what was in there made her look down and shake her head slowly. Her voice would crack and lose its clarity sometimes if asked about it. Most times, though, she'd end up thinking about something Kosmos had said about knowing when to wait. Good beer required a lot of waiting. And sometimes you won't even know exactly what it is you're waiting for until it gets here..."but you vait."

For her part, Miss Celie adjusted her dress, walked across the road to the little white house, closed the door and did just that.

CHRISTMAS
1962

MRS. CECELIE SPOETZL

WITH THIS PLAQUE WE YOUR EMPLOYEES WISH TO EXPRESS OUR APPRECIATION FOR THE GOOD-WILL AND GENEROSITY YOU HAVE EXTENDED TO US THROUGHOUT THE MANY YEARS

EMPLOYEES
SPOETZL BREWERY

THE FIRST AND SOLE BREWERY PROPRIETRESS IN THE U.S.A.

ABOVE: Goodwill and generosity were two ingredients that Miss Celie believed in.

LEFT: Miss Celie's house, across the road from the brewery.

In the 40's and 50's, the uninitiated may have thought they'd found the landing spot of Noah's Ark and not a brewery.

LEFT: Miss Celie hired
John Hybner in '66.
He later became brew-
master until 2005. He
wore different clothes
by then, though.

RIGHT: You don't
become brewmaster
overnight: John working
hard, filling kegs.

CHAPTER 6

THE AUSTIN THING: PART I

★ A FUNNY THING ★
HAPPENED
ON THE WAY TO THE
ARMADILLO

1966 – 1976

Our hometowns, with some exceptions, hold special tugs on our souls. And often the tug is more powerful and deeper felt because our destinies lay elsewhere and we have to leave those towns in search of said destinies. We never leave them truly, though.

Sinatra was New Jersey to the core (Hoboken, wasn't it?) but the Sinatra we knew was of Los Angeles and Las Vegas and, to a lesser extent, New York. Still, Hoboken rode with him through it all.

Chester Nimitz left Fredericksburg to find his fame on the Pacific. And more recently, Lance Armstrong, after a youth in Plano and then Austin, still wouldn't be Lance Armstrong were it not for France and a certain annual competition nobody this side of the pond much cared about until he went there. But he did, and so we do.

Plano Lance was one thing, but Austin Lance was entirely another, and in going to Austin, his eyes were widened to places far beyond and things that could be done elsewhere.

It is—as many a strip-mall-raised Texas child has learned—a unique kind of town, Austin. Janis Joplin, who couldn't draw flies in Port Arthur, found the truth of that at Kenneth Threadgill's place, thence later still in San Francisco, and later still…everywhere.

The number of people who've adopted Austin as a second hometown over the years could fill—well—Austin. And as residents and unwilling participants in the rolling gridlock of I-35 would be quick to tell you, it is now pretty much filled up to capacity and a good measure more.

But fame has its price, and lots of fame has been made in Austin…or at least it has begun there. And as the name on the label always clearly indicated, Shiner was where home, family and the neighbors resided and likely always would be for the beer that bore the town's name. But as the changes of the late '60s and early '70s swept through the rest of the country, just down the road Austin was becoming something far different than it was before. By sheer force of proximity, the Austin counterculture's love for things "natural" combined with the yearning of all those who worked at the brewery to share

their beloved nectar, meant that Shiner had a date with Texas' weirdest town that would leave both of them forever changed.

Unlike a lot of those pilgrimages to Austin at the time, this one didn't take place in a VW bus with flowers on it, but just as it always had—in the back of the truck Joe Green, Cracker and Lonnie would take to Austin on their delivery runs each week.

And much as the changes taking place throughout the country were having a polarizing effect between young and old, this same phenomenon was subtly happening to Shiner beer. Shiner Special Export, the brand that constituted 85 or 90 percent of the brewery's output, was mostly what Cracker and company delivered to Austin and throughout Central Texas. This was the nectar favored in the German and Czech domino halls, at the small-town festivals and by the ones old enough to remember Kosmos. Most beers were going lighter, though. Even so, in the kind of defiance that would make even old Kosmos proud, Shiner also put out a "bock" beer a couple of times each year—which always did particularly well in the capital, a foreshadowing indicative of very much bigger things to come.

It only makes sense that bock did well in Austin. Dating back even to the longhairs of the 1800s, the town that was Stephen F. Austin's namesake had always been a little different than the rest of the state. Travis County had voted against secession in the Civil War. In the years thereafter, it had always taken a generally contrarian's point of view in terms of things political and philosophical. The founding of The University of Texas in 1883 had only served to cement this fact and attract freer thinkers from elsewhere as well. By the 1950s and '60s, it was said that once you got thirty miles outside of Austin, you'd find yourself firmly back in Texas. It was true, too.

So it was that the upheavals and protests fomented by the Vietnam War would find their first Texas expressions in Austin, as well. The signs had always been there, but by May of 1971 when the newly constructed L.B.J. Presidential Library was dedicated on the U.T. campus, the signs were there literally, held by hundreds, if not thousands, of anti-war student protestors. The old Texas in the '40s-style Stetson hat of L.B.J. and company versus the new Texas in bandanas and shoulder-length hair.

I was there that day, on a field trip with my fifth-grade class from Berta May Pope Elementary in Arlington and had never seen such a thing as a hippie, outside of the *CBS Evening News with Walter Cronkite*. I certainly didn't know such a thing existed in Texas, but on that day I had my horizons broadened considerably further than my teachers had ever intended. There were speeches by political figures from D.C. and elsewhere, including the honoree himself. There were heckled words with meanings of which I had only fuzzy notions and tear gas, too, according to some. I could tell you nothing in particular about the event other than the fact I saw real hippies and real protest signs laying on the grass near 24th Street as we made our way back to the buses that would return us to our insulated little world in Arlington.

Texas wasn't just one thing anymore. Of course, it never had been in reality, but even in the eyes of those who thought they knew what Texas was and what all the people were like, even in those eyes there was now an old and a new and they

tourists still made their visits to the hospitality room for post-tour beers and conversation. But the makeup of this group was changing. In amongst the cowboy hats and old German and Czech accents, you were now just as likely to see longish hair, cut-off jeans and sandals.

Of course the folks in Shiner weren't demographers, trend analysts or even particularly adept marketers, they were just people who loved their beer and gladly welcomed anyone who shared that passion. And back in Austin, that upward-aimed rocket ship was about to have some extra provisions loaded on board for the ride.

IN AMONGST THE COWBOY HATS AND OLD GERMAN AND CZECH ACCENTS, YOU WERE NOW JUST AS LIKELY TO SEE LONGISH HAIR, CUT-OFF JEANS AND SANDALS.

---

were each going in very different directions. For me, the direction was north and back home to a suburban existence straight out of "King of the Hill." But as of that day, I knew I'd be coming back. I wanted to be in this place called Austin that was so foreign to what I'd experienced till then. For L.B.J., it was back to his ranch in Stonewall for the final year and a half of his life. For Austin, it was straight up, with an unmistakable shimmy to the left.

Back in Shiner, a new brewmaster, Chester Terpinski, had been brought in around '68 by a man from New Braunfels, Archie Ladshaw, who was a dynamite maker by trade (yes, I'm serious) and had taken the brewery over from Mr. Bigler. Domino games continued on, and the occasional groups of

Michael Smith and Phil Vitek were hippies. They'd gotten their degrees from The University but found little in their chosen fields of study that motivated them for the realities of postgraduate life. They'd partnered up in the running of a bar for a while and came to know the Shiner distributor out of New Braunfels who serviced the Austin market, as well. Outside of there and the other little German towns that could be counted on for good Shiner business, their distributor friend didn't see much of a future for this "old German drink," so he made a proposal to Michael and Phil.

"You boys take over the payments on this old truck and the equipment I have, and I'll throw in the Shiner distributorship for nothing," he'd half-seriously blurted out one afternoon.

ABOVE: Austinites and Shinerites bond over a common interest: Shot in the old hospitality room at the brewery. (photo courtesy of John Jennings)

Upon inspection, the truck certainly didn't look like much, nor any of the other stuff for that matter, but they chewed on the idea for a while and then decided to take him up on his offer.

Yes, Michael and Phil were hippies, but they were also house dwellers and people who had to pay bills. A beer distributorship, with the ability to sell beer in a town like Austin, seemed as good a way as any to do it, and it just might be fun. Even if it was that old German codger's beer, it was still, after all, beer, and it was cheap. Something always of much importance in the usually uncertain world of counterculture finances. Within a few months, they had acquired a no-longer-needed warehouse on 4th Street and begun a trip, the destination of which nobody saw coming.

It was 1972, and Austin's reputation of being a Berkeley in the center of one of the nation's most conservative states was daily becoming more well-established. The Armadillo World Headquarters was becoming nationally known and the Austin Opry House, Antone's, Threadgill's and the likes were bringing in an eclectic variety of acts from both coasts who spread the gospel of Austin to all those who would hear of it in their other venues. In any given month, you could see Frank Zappa, Commander Cody and His Lost Planet Airmen, Waylon Jennings, Muddy Waters, The Mahavishnu Orchestra and, of course, Willie Nelson, Jerry Jeff Walker and Michael Murphey before there was a "Martin" added to the middle of his name. And that was just at the Armadillo.

And as weird as that combination may now sound, what was weirder was the aggregation of people such venues were collecting. Hippies, cowboys, cowboys who looked like hippies, hippies who looked like cowboys, nerds (before there really was such a term), funky older Austinites who didn't have the hair but did have the politics of the counterculture, organic evangelists, the regular kind of fire-and-brimstone evangelists and just about any cocktail of any part or all of the above, could be found in the Armadillo and elsewhere on any given night.

Smith and Vitek's years as both participants and proprietors of the music and bar scene in Austin had given them backstage passes to this anthropological gumbo. Outside of the initial *Star Wars* cantina outlandishness of the scene, one of the first observations of anyone witnessing early 1970s Austin was that pretty much all these people drank beer. Here, however, cultural divides didn't erase so easily. There were the older folks drinking Schlitz or Miller High Life or Budweiser. There were the cowboys drinking the same or maybe Coors or

Lone Star, and then there were the hippies, whose inclination for things natural often directed them towards Shiner with its lack of artificial additives of any kind.

Beyond that, Shiner was clearly "non-corporate," "local," and (here's that word again), it was cheap. And though most of its drinkers didn't know the full extent of the Shiner story, it was still seen as a bit of the underdog and outsider—another thing the counter-culture found not at all counter to its values.

The fact that the two guys who ran the distributorship wore cut-offs and T-shirts as their on-duty attire didn't hurt either. Michael and Phil were well aware of all this and were happy to do business with those who appreciated the way they wanted to do business.

Friday afternoon parties were known to break out at "the dock" of the Shiner warehouse in Austin that would run well

FAR LEFT: Austin flows into Shiner, and vice versa. (photo courtesy of John Jennings)

LEFT: Mr. Siems, who ran the hospitality room well into the 80s, serving up cold beers and warm conversation in the old hospitality room.

into the night, and sales direct to the public (which were still legal at the time) took off. A friend of Michael and Phil's, also a hippie, with a penchant for driving around town in an old hearse with a limo driver's hat atop his T-shirt, cut-offs and (when he wore shoes at all) flip-flopped feet, was hired on part-time to do impromptu deliveries and make runs to the brewery for pickups and to get Smith and Vitek to distributor meetings.

In fact, it was in the guise of the hearse with the hippie driver with the limo cap that the little town of Shiner got its first glimpse of just what was happening to their beloved offspring over there in Austin. It was at a gathering for the distributors in Shiner, a fairly nondescript, if not dignified, event where the sight of the hippies in the hearse made it known that something was up.

Similar events were no doubt playing out all over the country where a daughter, newly sent off to college, brought a new boyfriend back home to meet the parents. Said boyfriend's

brews to make it more attractive to the palates of the younger beer drinkers. He made trips to Austin. He talked to the club goers and bar owners. Safe to say, he probably even sat in a few of those places for more than an hour or two for purely research purposes.

Like a geologist looking for a big strike of oil, John knew there was something there, it was just a matter of how to most effectively get there, while causing the least amount of damage to the environment—in other words, the oldsters.

Up until that time, "Special Export," a dark and fairly heavy beer (what a lot of people called "old German's beer") made up most of the brewery's output. You can, of course, imagine the potential minefields afoot at the very thought of messing with the recipe, but Mr. Hybner knew survival—in an age of corporate consolidation and buyouts—would depend on appealing to a younger group of people. Thus, the flagship brand went from "Special Export" to "Shiner Premium." Were people mad? Yes. There were some of the harder-boiled old ones who upped and quit the beer out of sheer principle. There was much arguing and controversy amongst the hard-core and

NATURALLY AGED · NATURALLY BETTER

long hair and less-than-preppy disposition was often a cause for great parental alarm or, at the very least, concern. In Shiner, too, there were all those emotions, but there was also the realization that beer was being sold in a far larger place and in far larger numbers than anyone had ever seriously thought about. Enough so, that "eccentricities," be they of hair-length or vehicle preference, could be overlooked. Not since the protests at the dedication of the L.B.J. Library had the differences between "old Texas" and "new Texas" been so graphically on display. But in this instance, at least, the representatives of said groups were far more willing to get along.

These extraterrestrials from Shiner of Austin clearly intended no harm and, in fact, wanted the same things the folks in Shiner wanted. Their methods were just a little… different. John Hybner, who'd taken over as brewmaster from Chester Terpinski, was as taken aback as anyone by the strange happenings 90 miles to the west. He, like Michael and Phil, knew there was not just weirdness, but potential sales there. Over the course of the early '70s, he thought long and hard about little things he could devise with the formulation of the

talk of Mr. Kosmos doing loop-de-loops in his place of rest, but most of that talk went on where Shiner mattered to people, and up until very recently Shiner hadn't meant a damn to enough people to fill a telephone booth or a VW Microbus. And now that some of those people who drove such things were showing some interest, why not try to appeal to them even more?

Fact is, given Mr. Kosmos' propensity for driving out into the countryside, chatting up the locals and always being quick with a cold one from the back of his old Ford coupe, he probably would have been more approving than you might think. He was always at his happiest when the most people possible were enjoying the fruits of his craft, so the mere thought of people a few more fence posts down the road enjoying his beers would probably have the old man singing rather than spinning. Maybe the formula had changed a little, but the mission was still the same.

Funny thing is, the brewery did keep making special batches of Bock a couple times a year. Some might say that it was to merely appease those who'd been put off by the demise of Special Export. And though Bock was certainly not the same as Special Export, it was darker and heavier than Shiner Premium. It certainly ran counter to every other trend going on in the beer business at the time. And they were selling the hell out of it in Austin.

Michael and Phil saw the bump in sales every time a new batch came out. It was still—in terms of the big boys—a boil on a gnat's buttocks, but they'd gotten to a place where you could actually use the word "growth" in the same sentence with the word "sales." They'd hosted some pretty damn fine parties too. The broken-down equipment they'd gotten, along with the afterthought of a beer distributorship had turned into quite the little cottage business for the guys, but the thought of owning their own restaurant remained a dream of both men. Changes in the state liquor laws now meant you couldn't own both a distributor's license and an "on-premise" restaurant or bar license, so in 1976 they decided to sell the distributorship and later open what would become an Austin institution in its own right—The Texas Chili Parlor on Lavaca Street.

Many years later, they sold that too, and did well from it. The one thing neither of them ever relinquished was Austin. Both of them still live there, though Michael spends half the year there and half the year in Maine. You can make wagers, if you like, as to which half is spent where. The day I sat with them at Threadgill's on Riverside, eating lunch and looking at old Armadillo posters and artwork, they told me they still "dabble in this and that." Investments in once-cheap houses around town have served them well, and they both have the look of men who've been there, done that, and lived to tell about it.

The Austin they knew then and that I discovered on a fifth-grade field trip is a very much different place now. The fact that we were just half a block or so from where the old Armadillo had created a whole new music world only underlined that fact. A hotel, like any you'd see in any of a thousand other places, covers the space now. Or maybe it's a parking lot. But this is not to say the Austin that is there now is not a wonderful place in spite of losses it may have incurred. It is. What it was then and what it remains to this day is a place where the unlikely gets its start. The town's sheer attractiveness brings the audience in for such starts,

and then things go on from there. We know it mostly for the musicians who came from the little towns and found in Austin a place that was not scared to let them become what they would become. A bigger stage? Yes, certainly, but more particularly, it's a freer stage. The kind of place that found it not at all strange to have Waylon Jennings play the same venue as Frank Zappa. But that freethinking applied to other endeavors, as well. Be they the written word, making computers, riding a bicycle or—thank the Good Lord—making a good beer.

And among all the wonderful hard-to-fully-quantify things Austin is, first and foremost, it's a place more than any other where people can truthfully say, "I knew them when..." Michael Smith and Phil Vitek can certainly say that about that little beer from Shiner. Moreover because they "knew Shiner when...," a whole lot more of us can say, "We know it now."

ARMADILLO BEER GARDEN

LEFT: The Armadillo World Headquarters. ABOVE: Back when things started getting weird: Armadillo World Headquarters and some of its improbable collection of pilgrims.
BELOW: There were even a couple of fellows by the name of Jerry Garcia and Doug Sahm that enjoyed Shiner from time to time (Thanksgiving, 1976).
(Photos courtesy of Ed Wilson, taken by Burton Wilson).

Shiner

Bock

Premium

Beer

BREWED FROM PUR
ARTESIAN WELL WA

NET CONTENTS
12 FL. OZ.

BEER BREAK

BEFORE THERE WAS WILLIE AND WAYLON, THERE WAS WILLIE AND HYBNER.

In much the same way you can't talk too long about Austin without uttering the word "Shiner," you can't help but include the name "Willie," the town's best known citizen. Matter of fact, the ubiquitousness of Shiner and Willie around town follow roughly the same timeline. Pretty much ever since the early '70s both were very likely to be seen in any number of places you went. And, boy, were there places to go. Certainly Austin, Shiner and even Willie were nowhere near the size any of them are now, nor did anyone foresee the coming boom for each.

Maybe it was like hanging out with the Rat Pack before they were really known as such. And so it was that in 1973 a meeting was arranged between brewmaster John Hybner, brewery owner Archie Ladshaw and Willie at Scholz's Garten. Even as well-known as Willie was becoming around town and in other parts of the country, Archie still had to ask Hybner who this guy was that they were meeting. He even went so far as to write "Willie" down on his hand to ensure he didn't forget his name.

Over time, Willie—an enthusiastic and skilled domino player—caught wind of similar traits in his acquaintance Hybner. Eventually Willie issued a challenge to John through the guys at the Shiner warehouse in Austin. Once the details were worked out, John was summoned to Willie's studio where they played one another in the best of five games.

As Hybner recalls, "Willie said, 'If you win, you get my bus. If I win, I get the brewery.'" Hybner explained the brewery wasn't his to bet, but he would take the bus.

In the end, he could have bet the brewery and driven away in a pretty legendary vehicle. Hybner won.

Then again, John brought the beer. And Willie seems to have done all right in spite of the loss.

A cold Shiner Spezial Leicht shot in Maeker's in Shiner, Texas.

CHAPTER SEVEN

THE AUSTIN THING: PART 2

"YOUR BIGGEST DRINKER JUST DIED."

1976-1989

Now this would be the place where the story could have taken a bad turn and seen Shiner go the way of The Armadillo and others into the shadows of great memories of what Austin "used to be like." But in Austin in 1976 there was certainly no shortage of those with an eye for the unusual. There was certainly no shortage of hippies, either. Bob Leggett and Marshall McHone, like their predecessors, were hippies. Of course, in 1976, such a description fit—at least in surface terms—no less than half the population. Just being cool-looking guys who didn't spend a lot of money on haircuts was nowhere near good enough to become nursemaids to a brand-new bouncing baby phenomenon.

For what it was worth, Bob was freshly armed with a biology degree from St. Edward's University—something he'd gotten in the spring of '76. What he found during the ensuing summer months was that said degree wasn't worth a lot. For the most part, he and Marshall, similarly armed to take on a world that didn't really exist, hung around town and tried to figure out what they wanted to do. No doubt in a preemptive effort to avert a case of move-back-in-itis, Bob's dad mentioned a business that he and a buddy were looking at—a business that needed somebody to run it.

The business, of course, was the Shiner distributorship. Maybe it was old Saint Gambrinus again, but Michael and Phil had fortuitously gotten in contact with somebody who knew somebody who knew Bob's dad, who knew Bob needed a way to make a living. The idea was intriguing to Bob and Marshall, especially when told Bob's dad and his partner would finance the deal. For $75,000, they purchased the distributorship Michael and Phil had gotten in '72 for not much more than the willingness to take on the payments on some aging equipment.

It was one of those rare deals in which everybody walks away from the table feeling good.

Bob and Marshall took over the old warehouse facility on 4th St. and for the first few months just focused on getting the lay of the land and becoming familiar with the customers. Lawrence "Speedy" Beal came out from Shiner as he always did, but did so more frequently to help with the transition and maybe school the new guys with some beer business wisdom, such as it was at the time.

"Zero times a million is still zero," was one of the first things Speedy had told the guys when they'd first met. Speedy had said it in an effort to impart the importance of trying to make a little profit on every case you can.

"Being new like we were, we were anxious to get into places that weren't carrying Shiner, so there was always the temptation to give a lot of freebies and offer better deals," Leggett remembers.

"Speedy just wanted to make sure we didn't get overly enthusiastic and give away the farm in hope of new business. Shiner was selling for around $5 a case at the time, way below the premium beers, so we took his words to heart. Anytime the other brands would up their prices, we'd increase ours by just a few pennies more to make up the gap a little. Nothing major, but just a little bit here and a little bit there, so we might have a little bit to put back into the brand," he recalls. "And it was only when the other guys raised their prices first. We were just trying to keep up and maybe put a little money back into the thing. We were never trying to take advantage of anybody."

We weren't trying to get rich, certainly; we were just trying to get ourselves up onto a little more level playing field, that's all. And even with our little increases over and above what the other guys took, Shiner was still great beer at a great price. We just made sure that we never got greedy. Speedy woulda told us about that, too."

In the fall of '77 a college friend of Bob and Marshall's who'd worked his way through school as a bank teller came to work, bringing the official company roster of Shiner of Austin to a grand total of three. Things were going well enough that Bob and Marshall bought out Bob's dad and his friend and were officially no longer working with house money.

Sad reality probably made this next incident even more memorable. Shortly after becoming full owners and managers of the company, Bob one day found himself at a regular and fairly reliable account who'd just recently reduced his order by a case per week. Understandably concerned, and fighting for every can or bottle they could sell, Bob inquired of the reason for the recent reduction of the bar's Shiner order.

"How come you knocked your order down by a case?" Bob asked over a beer one afternoon.

"Ya biggest drinker died," came the all-to-direct response. Here again the dichotomy of Shiner's two very different fan-bases was brought to life (or maybe we should say, "after-life").

"Say again?" Bob responded. "I said your biggest drinker died," the bar owner reiterated.

sales. This, clearly, was where the future was at, and that was easy to see in the clubs and bars in Austin. Places like the Wheatsville Co-op, The Deep Eddy Cabaret, Dirty Martin's, The Hole In The Wall, The Armadillo World Headquarters and others were among the big accounts of the time, and there the thirst for Bock seemed to have no end in sight.

Thus you can understand the alarm felt by Bob and Marshall when Speedy casually mentioned to them one day that the brewery was thinking about discontinuing Bock. Crazy as that may sound looking back from our perch well into the 21st Century, you must remember the hugeness of the Austin thing and what it could become was not yet nearly understood by the folks back in Shiner. It was still the old way there—and it's a good thing they never lost that way of looking at things—but the combination of Bock and Austin was getting ever nearer the point of combustion, and only Bob and Marshall and a few others were close enough to see the first sparks. Eventually, they managed to convince everybody there was a big future for

---

...looking back from our perch well into the 21st Century, you must remember, the hugeness of the Austin thing and what it could become was not yet nearly understood by the folks back in Shiner.

"That ol' man with the black safety glasses and the straw hat. One that used to sit over there ever' day lookin' at the paper and watchin' the *Perry Mason* reruns. Passed away two weeks ago. He was good for two cases a month, solid, like clockwork. Same number ever' day. Regular as a Milk of Magnesia commercial. Gonna miss him," the bar owner continued.

Dying drinkers never look good on any sales projection chart, and though Bob and Marshall didn't have such luxuries, they did have good business sense. They also knew that stories from bar owners about the passing of customers—while touching in the way it made things personal—certainly didn't bode well for their plans of growing the Shiner brand in Austin.

It was more of the dichotomy of old Texas versus new Texas that had started in the '60s, and it was a gap that was continuing to grow wider by the day. Shiner the town may have been only 90 miles to the east, but in terms of understanding the Austin phenomenon, there were days when it might as well have been a thousand miles away. Up to now, the semi-regular brewing and delivery of Bock to Austin was looked upon as a Godsend and could always be counted on to increase overall

Bock and even managed to get the brewery to brewing it on a full-time basis, which it did in 1978.

This is not to say that everyone in Austin could see what Bob and Marshall could see. At least, not yet. They remember clearly being laughed out of the Bean's Restaurant on Sixth Street in 1979 or '80, its proprietor unaware or uninterested in the subtle little changes that had over the course of the '70s taken the general perception of Shiner in Austin from "old German-geezer beer to that of a cool, darker-colored bock beer with a little bolder flavor to it."

The exact point at which water boils is certainly a very quantifiable temperature, yet in witnessing that process, it's never easy to say precisely when you've gone from non-boiling to boiling. Let's just say that in 1979 and '80, the bubbles were really getting started.

In '79, Shiner of Austin had grown from an operation of three people who did pretty much everything to a more respectable group of 10 or 12 people who did pretty much everything. Outgrowing the old rickety warehouse and the sight of so many parties on 4th Street, they moved into

another, larger warehouse on East 7th Street. One of the first things to make the move was the much-loved, well-used and nearly legendary "beer machine" that had held court over the operation since the beginning. An old Dr Pepper machine, it had been converted to hold ice-cold Shiners and drop them lovingly into the hands of anyone who deposited a quarter into the slot. Quirky as the beer it distributed and the people into whose hands it dropped its contents, the beer machine was symbolic of the way Shiner had worked even back in Kosmos' days. Take what little you have, and find a way to make it work a little while longer—the goal always being that of getting more Shiner out there to more people.

As the '80s picked up and the hippies shared more time with the punks in the exploding Austin music scene, the little distributorship that sold the beer from the little brewery was becoming quite a little beer machine in its own right. The Armadillo had closed down and been demolished for a hotel in 1980, but the music scene grew nonetheless, proving that Austin music, like Shiner, had roots that were strong enough to survive the loss of any given branch. The *Urban Cowboy* movie craze, in 1980 and '81 had taken over much of the country and Texas especially, but this didn't really fit in with the Austin way of looking at things, so its effects were minimal at best. People there had always "danced country at The Broken Spoke" and the encouragements of John Travolta and a Hollywood movie about a honky-tonk in Houston were

unlikely to make Austin people do things much differently than they were already doing.

Ironically enough, the craze the movie did create in other parts of the country led to the introduction of "Gilley's Beer"— Gilley's being the name of the club in Houston where much of the movie had been shot. That beer was brewed under contract at the brewery in Shiner. Most people never knew that, and the brand lasted only a few years as is typical of such Hollywood trends, but it was an indicator that despite the growing successes in Austin, Shiner overall was still struggling to survive. Contract brewing, or the brewing and packaging of another company's beer (think "moonlighting") was a way to enhance income and make ends meet in the lean times, which were more and more the norm as the '80s wore on. Even with the contract brewing and the popularity of Shiner Bock in Austin, the brewery was operating way under capacity.

In July of 1984, a group of investors from Houston, including the chairman of Foley's department stores, bought the brewery with the intention of upping its output and doing a better job of marketing and promotion. Much of the problem was still the fact that Shiner was two brands going very different directions. The "old Shiner" (Premium) continued to suffer the scourge of the "dying drinker," yet was still the brew the folks around the brewery knew best. The "new Shiner" (Bock) was all that was going on in Austin. Something that, for the most part, was left to Leggett and McHone to promote and figure out on their own.

There was no MBA on staff, no highly thought-through marketing plan, but being in Austin meant Leggett and McHone had access to something few other cities in the country had in such volume: artists—both of the musical and the graphic nature. In 1980, they'd asked some friends and friends of friends to paint the delivery trucks. Don Cauley, the boyfriend of one of the ladies who worked at the distributorship, had learned his craft in the Armadillo days. He was one of the first invited to paint a truck. What emerged were the famous "cloud trucks," a purely "Austintatious" interpretation of Shiner and its relationship with the Austin mindset. First and foremost, it was art. Art that just happened to serve secondarily as a billboard, making its way around town day after day. Paintings of local musicians were also included on the trucks, which throughout the '80s endeared themselves to the locals much as the old "moonlight tower" street lamps still

ABOVE: The family and friends of the Shiner of Austin distributors. Bob Leggett and Marshall McHone are pictured on the bottom left.

RIGHT: Mickey Gilley's Beer was brewed at the Spoetzl Brewery in the lean times, along with some other local beers.

seen around town or the nightly flight of the bats down at the Congress Avenue Bridge. It was advertising, but it was indigenous advertising that struck just the right chord with its audience. Eventually, Marcia Ball, Joe "King" Carrasco, Paul Ray and the Cobras and others were emblazoned on the sides of the trucks.

Then there was the kind of advertising money can't buy. In '81 a local group of bike and Shiner enthusiasts, who would get together and ride their bikes to Shiner for the free beer at the hospitality room, formalized their trek. Thus, G.A.S.P., or the Great Austin-Shiner Peddle was born. The popularity of the beer in Austin had now grown to the point where lack of promotional funds on the brewery's part was being made up for by grassroots efforts that didn't cost a dime.

In '88, Leggett asked Austin artist Micael Priest to do a poster about Shiner Bock that could be used for promotions and bar giveaways. What he came back with was the famous "Brewed With An Attitude" poster that would eventually come to represent the brand throughout the better part of the '90s.

But for all the good things happening in Austin, the "attitude" of the poster belied the trouble that continued to brew back in Shiner. Austin, as it always had been in so many other ways, was an anomaly. Austin was the place where the party was. It was the place you could forget about all your troubles. But as any weekend visitor to the place can tell you, eventually you have to go back to the problems of home. For Shiner, in 1988, those problems at home were many. Austin with its funky delivery trucks was the one bright cloud in an otherwise dismal picture. In Shiner there was not enough money for sorely needed upgrades or the kind of marketing that had gone on by improvisation at Shiner of Austin.

The ram on Micael Priest's poster had two horns.

Of course it did. Most rams do. And though he surely never considered the symbolism in this particular piece of art, it was almost as if he'd painted the beast from a biblical vision of revelation. The beast had two horns, but in the course of time one would overtake the other one. There was Bock and there was Premium, and as one had overtaken the other in Austin, that same thing would have to happen elsewhere.

Overly deep? Yeah, probably so. But as the Spoetzl Brewery got ready to celebrate its 80th anniversary, the situation harkened back to 1915, when the struggling Shiner Brewers Association found itself on hard times as well. The prospects of its continuing on looked dismal until an immigrant showed up on the scene, bought the place, and helped ensure that it would live to see many, much brighter days.

Of course, the idea of history repeating itself is mostly just a romantic notion far more common in fiction than real life. It almost seems too neat a way to tie a bunch of ragged ends up and make them into something prettier than what they were.

So what to make, then, of the fact that in '89 there was another immigrant hanging around Austin and watching from the wings? Yours truly, the storyteller, may long for something more original, less neat-and-tidy to tie up the hanging ends. The characters in said story, however, had no such aversions. All they knew was that the two Shiners shared one thing other than family lineage. For good or for bad, they both stood on the brink. The fate of everything Kosmos had built and those who came after him had nourished, was in danger of going the way so many other little breweries had gone.

By 1989, nobody had any inkling which way the drama would play out.

The new immigrant had an idea or two, though.

LEFT: The artwork of Micael Priest that launched the "brewed with an attitude" slogan.

RIGHT: Micael Priest painting the back of one of the Shiner of Austin trucks with fiddler extraordinaire Erik Hokkanen's portrait.

LEFT: A christening party, held at Threadgill's with young Erik Hokkanen, friends and a couple of Shiners.

RIGHT: Erik proceeds to shake things up a bit.

BEER BREAK

THE NICE THING ABOUT BEING A WHITE ELEPHANT IS NOBODY WANTS TO SWALLOW YOU.

Between 1950 and 1980, the market share of the U.S.' 10 largest breweries grew from 38% to 93%. A great deal of that growth came at the expense of the country's small, independent breweries, of which the Spoetzl Brewery was undoubtedly a proud—even defiant—member.

Lone Star, Pearl, Olympia, Rainier, Schmidt's...the list goes on and on of the many independent regional breweries which were swallowed up, resold, had their brewing operations moved elsewhere or were downright shut down during the corporate acquisition high-times of the last half-century or so.

Much of the later growth of the big breweries was fueled by the light beer revolution of the 1970s. The introduction of Miller Lite in 1976, thence the other light beers shortly thereafter left the breweries flush with cash to acquire rivals, increase their own brewing capacity and set themselves up better for the competitive years to come.

So what of the little brewery in Shiner? Why wasn't it just another in the long list of those swallowed up, never to be seen again? The answer again lies, as does so much about this quirky little place, in a big gurgling vat of irony. The years and years of being strapped for cash and literally holding things together with duct tape and whatever old equipment they could gather from defunct breweries, meant that most would-be suitors were scared away before the first date.

Certainly, the big brewers saw nothing they felt they could make use of. Even the medium-sized brewers were frightened by the smallness of the operation, the family nature of the business and relative isolation of the town itself.

Of course, these were the days before the microbrewery craze, during which the big brewers did their best to acquire smaller brewers with "character." But even then, the little brewery in Shiner seemed to present more problems than answers for any would-be pursuers. Bill Bigler, Archie Ladshaw, the dynamite maker, and even the group of businessmen from Houston who'd bought the brewery in '84 had all come in with good intentions but had never found the right combination of marketing and reinvestment to make things work like they should.

The big companies seemed to not think it was worth their time or investment.

So in a funny way, for all the lack of modern equipment, shortages of cash and small-town outlook over the years, we should all be eternally thankful. The little piece of beautiful property on Brewery Street, next to Boggy Creek, never got subdivided and turned into tract houses or, worse, paved over and never given a second thought.

And so it was still there in 1989, waiting for somebody who appreciated the property for what it was and, moreover, someone who saw the potential for what it could be.

A cold Shiner Hefeweizen shot in Scholz' Bier Garten in Austin, Texas.

CHAPTER 8

★ ANOTHER ★

IMMIGRANT
COMES TO
SHINER

1989 - 1999

Maybe the answer should have been obvious. Of course, it wasn't. The little brewery in Shiner had been founded by immigrants. It had been run by them through thick and thin up until '66. Since then, despite the efforts of many good people and the successes in Austin, things just hadn't been the same. Matter of fact, things had deteriorated to the point where bankruptcy was at hand.

Lots of other people had taken their shot; so maybe it was time to try turning it back over to an immigrant again. Maybe that was the missing piece. Of course, nobody in his right mind was suggesting that this was the solution in the late '80s. But then, sometimes the improbable solution is the right one. And, of course, improbable answers generally get far more consideration as the situation grows more desperate.

An immigrant to run an immigrant's brew? With the full blessings of hindsight, of course, it makes all the sense in the world. But in 1989 they didn't have the benefit of that in Shiner. Matter of fact, hope was almost as thin as the skin of the old copper brew kettle that was down to paper-thin and in danger of failing at any moment. And as the brew kettle went, so went the brewery.

It was a journey to San Antonio that had brought Kosmos his first introduction to Shiner and the little brewery. So, too, Carlos Alvarez had come in 1986. Like Kosmos, he'd grown up around the beer business, only in Acapulco as opposed to Bavaria. English was a second language for both, but each man spoke fluent beer. Carlos had gone to work for Cerveceria Modelo and risen to become the head of exports. Later he'd gone out on his own, moved to Texas and become the importer for Modelo in Texas and 24 eastern states. Much of Alvarez' teeth-cutting occurred on the streets of Austin in the early '80s. He, along with Bob Leggett and Marshall McHone, had sold the first bottle of Corona Extra in the United States in June of 1981. He named his fledgling company after the patron saint of all beer drinkers, Gambrinus.

If you've been with me on this little journey since way back in the '50s, you'll recall the article by Sig Byrd, the newspaper columnist from Houston, who wrote about Shiner in 1953. He'd said, "Shiner is a charming town, mostly because of the Spoetzl Brewery, which is protected by Saint Gambrinus, the patron of beer drinkers."

I don't know how you feel about such "coincidences," but I have always believed there are unseen things at work that we can never fully understand. In this case, a little otherwise unremarkable foreshadowing written years in advance that then disappears into a pile of yellow newsprint crammed into a box in the back of the old brewhouse. A little further digging yields another such "coincidence." Sig Byrd passed away in 1987. That same year, Carlos Alvarez made his first trip to Shiner to tell them he was interested in buying the place.

"So what?" you may reasonably ask. Well, it's just that I suppose I'm one of those people who like to at least entertain the notion that Mr. Byrd on his way out of this world mentioned to somebody while he was being in-processed into the next life that the little place in Shiner that Saint Gambrinus, the patron saint of beer, had been watching over was in need of a little extra blessing and that maybe somebody could poke around and check into things to see what could be done. I like to imagine that, unlike bureaucracy as it generally runs here on earth, somebody on the receiving end of Mr. Byrd's tip actually did look into the matter and saw that, "well, what do you know, there's this fellow calling his company Gambrinus, so maybe we'll just make sure and grease the skids a little so that this thing works out."

Maybe they checked with Kosmos, too. I'd imagine he'd have put in a vote for this Gambrinus guy as well.

But back on earth, the reality of it is, when Carlos first came calling, the owners, in an effort to get more money for the place, were about to make a private stock offering, so the timing wasn't right. End of discussion. Of course, Carlos' notion to buy the place hadn't come from some divine knock upside the head; it was a lot more ordinary than that. Having started his importing business in San Antonio that year and having worked with Leggett and McHone since the late seventies, he'd spent a lot of time in Austin. Being one of the country's best college towns, it was a great place to spot trends, watch people's behavior and just overall get a good feel for what might be happening in the wider market down the road. He was there, of course, on behalf of Modelo and its fledgling Corona Extra brand he was trying to get going in the U.S. But the one thing he kept noticing more than anything was the way Shiner Bock seemed to be gaining popularity. It was everywhere. And the more authentic the bar, the more likely it was to be there. Then he'd go 79 miles back down the road to San Antonio and—poof—Shiner was nowhere to be seen. Unfortunately, unless it got some more money to upgrade its duct tape and baling wire facilities, the brewery itself was well down the road to going "poof" and disappearing for good. Truth is, most people saw the brewery as a money pit out of which one could never expect to see any return.

Of course, Carlos Alvarez wasn't most people. He was different. Some might even say a little odd. Say this for him, though: he'd named his company correctly. If old Saint Gambrinus looked out for beer drinkers, he had nothing on Carlos. He wasn't a distributor; he was a watcher—a beerthro-pologist. He simply watched what people did and how they behaved when it came to beer. And unlike projected sales charts on an overhead screen or focus groups with "average consumers," he believed the only way you could tell what was going to happen with a beer brand was by actually sitting in the bars and restaurants and clubs and paying attention. Yeah, I know, you're thinking, "all right, sign me up, that's the job for me," but it's one thing to watch and another entirely to know what to do with your observations.

One other thing Carlos Alvarez was not. He was not a pessimist. Matter of fact, he was a full-on, unrepentant, glass (or in this case bottle) is half-full optimist. It takes one of those to do some of the things he'd already done by the late '80s. A lot of the folks at Cerveceria Modelo had thought he was crazy when he told them he wanted to package Corona Extra in the clear bottles and sell it in the States. And as those folks snickered, he and some other folks proceeded to turn a lightly regarded stepchild into Cinderella.

Still, even the optimist couldn't help noticing the drastic drop-off between Austin and San Antonio. The key, he figured,

was to find a way to get the things happening in Austin to start happening in some bigger places like San Antonio, Houston and Dallas. Then there was the price thing. Although Bob Leggett and Marshall McHone had done what they could over the years to bring Shiner up from the "dirt cheap" category,

---

Shiner did have something all those other brands longed for—character and a non-fabricated small town brewing tradition that meant something to people.

---

restore a little respectability and make a bit of money as well, Shiner Bock was still priced right along with the domestics. Given the way people were discovering it in Austin, Carlos wondered if you couldn't price it higher than premium beers, make enough money to put back into the brewery and even add to the perception of the beer's authenticity.

As much maligned as sitting on a barstool is in country songs and in certain church pulpits, one could certainly learn a thing or two while seated there. Especially if you had the notion, as Carlos Alvarez did, to not drink too much and pay attention to what was going on around you. He wasn't some

ABOVE: Carlos Alvarez saw something worth saving.

119

savant or visionary, he just did what a good number of us would be well-served to do. Sit down, kick back with a beer, and think, and maybe even plan a little bit. One has to think if old Saint Gambrinus felt it worthwhile to watch over the beer drinker, it wasn't because of the ones who over-partook and got into fights, it was for the ones who used their heads and not just their elbows.

Carlos' elbow was about to get all the exercise it needed anyway, from picking up the telephone.

About eight months after he'd first called the ownership group out of Houston that was running the brewery, they called back. The private stock offering they'd been hoping would raise

even think about it." In their eyes there was no way to ever turn things around at a little brewery like that.

There was, along with the skepticism of the outside world, the very real and understandable suspicion of the people who worked at the brewery. It was more than palpable when he went to the brewery to meet everyone and address them regarding his plans. Some thought him to be just another guy with a little money who wanted to play brewmaster. But Alvarez first and foremost was a sales guy. He enjoyed that part of the business and knew that what John Hybner was doing and had been doing since '72 was the right thing. He just wanted to increase the number of people who would taste his handiwork.

"People have suggested that I had a vision that anticipated the boom of the microbrewery business. Frankly, I didn't see that the microbrewing industry would grow anywhere near what it did."

---

much-needed cash, hadn't worked out. If Carlos was serious, they wanted to talk. He was. And they did. Of course, even with a small brewery, you don't just sit down over a couple of Shiners, throw a few numbers around, shake hands and grab the keys to your brand-new, old brewery that needs a little work under the hood and maybe has a little minor body damage. Even when Kosmos had first come to Shiner in 1914, there had been negotiations, finally resulting in an option to buy if he was able to get the place in shape and producing good beer.

Here, of course, the problem wasn't good beer. There was plenty of that. It was about putting money back into the place and marketing the beer they had in places where it had never been marketed. The brewery itself had pretty much been in less than ideal shape since even before Miss Celie had sold it. It was clear that turning the tide would take a lot of money. For Carlos' part, he had to figure out a price he could pay that would still allow him to do the things he felt needed doing to get the place off the mat and profitable. The better part of a year was spent in negotiations. By the end of 1989, they had a deal.

An immigrant would be running the brewery again.

Not long after, Carlos was on an airplane sitting next to a guy who worked with a New York brokerage firm. After Alvarez mentioned his association with Shiner, the broker got a strange look on his face. He told Carlos a client of his had asked him a few years before to look at Shiner as an investment possibility. The brokerage's answer, of course, had been, "Don't

Moreover, Alvarez wanted to set everyone at ease, but understandably, after three ownership changes in the previous 20 years, there was still, at the very least, a wait-and-see attitude and, at worst, downright doubt. And maybe that doubt only increased when one of the first things Gambrinus set about doing was—exactly what you wouldn't expect a troubled brewery to do—raising the price.

And before you start the chorus of boos and hisses and laments of greed, remember this: Shiner, in some places, was selling for less than it cost to make it—all in an effort to stay competitive with the big breweries and their domestic flagship beers. The way Alvarez saw it, that was suicide—a just very recently nearly completed suicide, one might add. Shiner would never be able to beat or even compete with those brands and make a good profit. Shiner did, however, have something all those other brands longed for—character and a non-fabricated small-town brewing tradition that meant something to people. And yes, he believed it was something people would pay a little extra for because they felt like they were getting a little something beyond the usual and outside the mainstream in return for their money.

There was another thing. This one, a lesson from Corona Extra.

Corona, in Mexico, is pretty much the ubiquitous, standard beer fare. Down there, it's the south-of-the-border equivalent of a can of Bud. In the States, however, Corona had been marketed as the beer that takes you back to your last trip down

to the beach in Cancun or Cozumel. You weren't just buying a beer; you were buying that feeling you got on vacation.

By the same token, people who lived in Dallas or Houston and, to a lesser extent, San Antonio looked forward to road trips to Austin and the fun that was to be had there. Shiner, since the early '70s had woven itself into that whole experience and now, not just for the old hippies, it was simply "that Austin beer" that brought with it all the memories and positive thoughts of a weekend getaway. Likewise, people in Dallas and Houston who hadn't been able to find it up to now, would pay a little extra for the "Austin-in-a-bottle factor." To them, Shiner was a "real beer," worth the extra money. Or so the thinking went anyway. And if that thinking was proven correct, there would at least be the money to sink back into the place and keep things going.

Pricing was also an important way to fend off national competition and defend Shiner's turf. In the end, it simply isn't practical to make a beer of the quality of Shiner and compete with the prices of the national brewers.

mix was another thing, though. When Alvarez acquired the place, the brewery's output was about 75% Shiner Premium and 25% Shiner Bock. Given the notion of selling Bock as a premium beer in Dallas, Houston and San Antonio, this would have to be turned on its ear. Certainly there were more than one or two upraised brows at the notion—especially when combined with the idea of raising the price to compete against premium rather than popular-priced domestic beers. More than a couple of "industry analysts" pooh-poohed the notion that Shiner could turn itself into a "specialty beer," but in the end, it didn't matter what they thought or what Alvarez thought. The good ol' impartial market would be the judge.

And so it was.

"People have suggested that I had a vision that anticipated the boom of the microbrewery business," Alvarez says. "Frankly, I didn't see that the microbrewing industry would grow anywhere near what it did. We were actually just trying to generate a specialty beer category within Texas without really knowing that something similar was going on in Washington

In 1993, Shiner reached a milestone: 1,000,000 cases sold for the first time ever in brewery history.

Moreover, Alvarez's visits to the town and the brewery had only served to reconfirm the importance of keeping the place open. Sure, it was the second biggest employer in town, but not nearly the size of the Kaspar Wire Works across the road, but its death would have been a huge blow to the morale of the town, not to mention what it would have done to the families of those who worked there—many for the second or third generation. There was also the matter that virtually all the little local breweries, so numerous a century before, had either been shuttered or swallowed up into their big acquirers, never to be heard from again. As a beer man and beer historian, the notion of this happening to the last little brewery in Texas was particularly troubling. But the best news was that if it was done right, he firmly believed Spoetzl could become profitable again and forget forever about contract brewing and the like. So, as he moved forward with his plan, those agreements were allowed to expire, opening up what he believed would be much-needed future capacity for Shiner.

There was no employee shake-up. The 40-something staff that made things go was a good one. Most had grown up in the town and were lifers. People were not the problem. The product

or Oregon or Massachusetts. We saw in Shiner Bock a dark beer with more character than a typical domestic selling well in Texas, a state where the light beer per capita consumption is the largest in the country. The idea of selling something different was what I saw in Shiner."

Sales nearly doubled from 1990 to 1992, going from 30,000 barrels to 53,000 barrels. Shiner Bock climbed to become the number three draft beer in Austin behind only Miller Lite and Budweiser. In Dallas/Fort Worth, Shiner grew by 90 percent in 1991, and 120 percent in 1992. By the end of '92, more than 80 percent of the brewery's production was Shiner Bock, an almost complete 180-degree turn from the day Alvarez had bought the place.

Oh yeah, there was one other little 180-degree-turn of some note: The brewery made a small profit. Stores in Houston that had once called Shiner "dead on arrival" and spent most of their time dusting the cobwebs off the beer were now moving 200 to 300 cases per month. There were myriad reasons for the turnaround; some are still to be addressed, but surely one of them was the long, hard look Alvarez and company took at the packaging. In the early '90s, each of the Shiner packages

LEFT: Things start shaping up with bottles flying on and off the shelves.

was evaluated and "cleaned-up" to ensure Shiner stood out on the shelves and yet still communicated the long heritage of Spoetzl. This would become an ongoing process over the coming years in contrast to the almost "afterthought" it had been up to now. Certainly what was in the bottle was the most important thing, but if you couldn't get somebody to at least pick up the bottle or the six-pack and take a look, there was little likelihood they'd ever know just how good the contents were. This as much as anything demonstrated why the Alvarez-Spoetzl marriage was such a nice match. The brewery was great at brewing, Alvarez and Gambrinus were great at recognizing great brewing when they saw it and leaving the brewers alone to do

---

It's a story that would ring of overdone fiction if it weren't for the simple fact the whole damn thing's true.

---

what they do best, while giving them the best tools possible to get the job done.

In 1993, Shiner reached a milestone: 1,000,000 cases sold for the first time ever in its history. In an effort to say thanks to all the folks in Shiner who'd stood by and stood firm during all the changes of the past three or four years, a "Thanks A Million" concert and celebration were thrown on the brewery grounds. Things were not only looking up, they had gone up, way up through the once-leaking roof of the old brewhouse, and people around town were taking notice too.

"He was our knight in shining armor," Myra Lampley, News Editor at the *Shiner Gazette* said of Carlos and the changes that had come about in just a few short years. The concert offered further proof of that. Certainly Myra, along with Managing Editor, Agnes Sedlmeyer had seen and reported on a whole bunch of changes at the brewery during their watch. Without a doubt, the *Gazette* had been invaluable in getting the news out about the concert and festival.

There was an ulterior motive to "Thanks A Million," though. With so many new drinkers, many had no idea there was a real place called Shiner. The concert was seen as a way to officially greet a whole lot of new friends and introduce them to the family, so to speak. From a purely marketing perspective, it was a great opportunity to reinforce one of Shiner's biggest brand benefits—real beer from a real town.

That and, of course, the fact that it would be one helluva lot of fun.

Being held in March, though, the weather was as iffy as the balance sheets had once been. Longtime Gambrinus employees remember the day of the concert dawning cold and rainy. February had been the wettest in recent memory in Central and South Texas, and the couple of days of respite March had brought was looking short-lived. Given such crummy conditions, everyone wondered just how many people would actually show.

Austin and San Antonio were experiencing flooding rains and as the morning wore on, it looked as if the concert might be a washout—literally.

And then, much in the fashion of Texas weather, Shiner was inundated with a deluge of its own. Carload after carload after truckload began descending on the place until somewhere between 8- and 9,000 souls had in a matter of hours grown the town four times its usual size.

Here you are welcome to draw any parallels you wish with the growth Shiner experienced during the '90s. Most all would certainly be appropriate. One very large group of people had experienced a day of great music and learned that, yes, Virginia, there was a Shiner, Texas.

For its part, the town of Shiner learned just how beloved its little brewery truly was—not to mention how quickly the store shelves of Howard's convenience store could be emptied of their contents.

But there was more change in the air and it would certainly amount to far more than just parties on the brewery grounds. In 1992, Alvarez took John Hybner, Spoetzl's brewmaster, and a brewing consultant on a tour of Germany and the Czech Republic to learn how the old breweries there had managed to modernize while remaining true to their traditional standards. Upon their return, plans were drawn up and construction soon began on a new brewhouse. The one single, paper-thin, ever-leaking copper brew tank bought secondhand in 1941, would be retired to a place of honor and new equipment would meet the growing demand.

ABOVE & RIGHT: Later to become Hefeweizen, Shiner built quite the buzz around this summertime treat with the Shiner Honey Wheat "Bee-hicles."

That nod to the past as the brewery looked to the future also took the form of a new beer. Kosmos Reserve (the first offering from the brewmasters with their new toys), a dark amber beer in appropriate tribute to the man who started it all, was introduced in 1993. It was not only a way to showcase the Old World talents that still ran the day-to-day brewing at Shiner; it was also yet another indication of the renewed vigor that was now flowing through the place.

Also in '93, Shiner began to move beyond Texas, becoming available for the first time in 14 states. People hundreds of miles away would now be able to share in the joys of Kosmos' little brewery. Better still, expatriate Texans began finding, much to their surprise, that a long cool drink of Texas could be had even far from home.

The "Thanks A Million" concert of 1993 morphed into "Bocktoberfest" in 1994, and life just kept on getting sweeter (or darker), depending on how you want to look at it. Shiner even began running its first radio commercials with Texas musicians like Robert Earl Keen, Jimmy LaFave and Ray Wylie Hubbard. 1994 also saw the introduction of Shiner's first ale, Shiner Hefeweizen, an unfiltered wheat beer brewed with orange and lemon peels and a bit of honey (it was originally called Shiner Honey Wheat).

By 1995, the surest sign of success was bestowed upon the Shiner resurgence when Anheuser Busch introduced its "Ziegenbock" brand in Texas. Bock had arrived, even in the eyes of the big brewers. They saw something special was happening and wanted to be a part of it. As for Shiner, production was now at 134,000 barrels, more than three times what it had been in 1989. Construction was completed on the new brewhouse, and operations began there as well. There were also new brew kettles and a quality assurance lab to better monitor the product.

Perhaps the most amazing thing about the new brewhouse, tanks and packaging equipment was the change required of its human operators. Remember, at the time, the 40 or so employees were people who'd been working at the brewery a long, long time, doing things the same way for sometimes 40 or 50 years. Many of these folks were in their 60s or 70s at the time. No matter. Everyone simply relearned their job and in most cases did so without complaint.

The only real glitch came when it was time to make the final switch from the old brewhouse to the new. Necessarily, there would be a period of a few days when no beer would come off the line, due to the switch. It was critical that the work happen as quickly as possible to ensure no shortages. As luck would have it, one of the key moments in the changeover came during the weekend, and local electricians were needed to help complete the work. In a moment that could happen only in Shiner, the critical work had to wait. Deer season had just begun that week, and all the electricians within close proximity were gone hunting.

There were some hardheads who claimed rather passionately that the taste of the beer changed with the arrival of the new upgrades. No amount of assurances to the contrary, it seemed, would change their minds. Most likely, the "change" they were tasting was simply the result of consistency and quality control—two ingredients that had been sorely missing for a number of years.

The fervent claims of old hardheads aside, John Hybner marveled at the new facility, built from the trips he and Carlos had made to Germany and the Czech Republic a few years before. "The only 'automatic' device in the old brewhouse was the thermometer, with an arrow that would rise as the temperature increased in the kettle," Hybner recalled. For his part, he was now free to concentrate on the finer points of the brewer's art and showcase his talents rather than just worry about how to hold things together and keep the place running another day.

The new 200-barrel brewhouse, while certainly state-of-the-art, was built in such a way to ensure it remained true to the art Kosmos had begun all those years before. The main goal was to increase capacity without compromising in any way the standards that had been set at the very beginning. There was a groan here and there that all this progress looked "just a little too pretty." There were some worries that all this success might make the brewery get a "little too big for its britches." Of course, progress or growth of any kind elicits those kinds of worries, but no one had ever set out to make the brewery any different than what it always had been. That, after all, was its strength. And yes, there would be building, there would be marketing too. But none of it would ever begin without a good long look back, to determine if it was right.

Elvis may have left the building, as the famous line goes. Kosmos, however, never really has, no matter which building we're talking about here. Matter of fact, the old immigrant was consulted often by the new immigrant in all that was done, not via Ouija board or séance, but by just looking back and taking good hard looks at the ways he had approached things.

LEFT: Carlos and the boys enjoy some cold ones after a hard day's work at Bocktoberfest.

THANKS A MILLION

And fortunately, there were still people around town and at the brewery in whose minds Kosmos' feelings about things were still as clear as the old painting of him hanging in the hospitality room.

Distribution, was, of course, Carlos Alvarez' area of expertise. It was also the area in which he saw the biggest opportunities for improvement. The notion of increasing distribution and visibility through partnerships with wholesalers in Dallas, Fort Worth, Houston, San Antonio and elsewhere meant change—sometimes very difficult and painful—was inevitable. Shiner's "mom and pop" way of doing things all through its history had—while contributing to its legend—greatly limited any opportunities for expansion.

In the old days, the attitude was "Okay - here's the beer, come pick it up." Once the product left the brewery, Shiner had felt its job was done. The new way was - here's the beer, it comes with a business plan, marketing and field sales support to help reach common goals. This "new way" understood the beer wholesaler and the challenges of the retail business as well as the drinkers.

The trade-off was—as there usually is when any business moves forward—the fact that long, ongoing relationships inevitably came to an end.

Even in Austin, where much of the whole crazy trip of the last 30 years had started, there was a changing of the guard. Shiner of Austin made the difficult decision to sell the Austin distributorship to Capitol Beverage in 1996. If there were growing pains, surely this was chief among them. Yet the fact remained, without the delivery capability, without the leverage to get Shiner more space in the stores and more tap handles in the bars, all the great things that had come about since 1989 would be for naught.

Turning to the fun (in other words, "beer") side of things, the brewery continued introducing more styles and flavors of beers. "Winter Ale" a Dunkelweizen (dark wheat beer) was the first Shiner seasonal, making its debut in October of 1997, and Shiner "Summer Stock," a Kolsch beer fashioned after the traditional beer style in Cologne, Germany, was introduced in the spring of '98.

Though not a "new" beer, Shiner repackaged Shiner Premium, renaming it "Shiner Blonde." This was not done as mere marketing sleight of hand. The fact of the matter was, in spite of all the good things happening with Bock, and maybe in some ways because of Bock's success, Shiner Premium had languished and just about fallen off the face of the map—especially in the newer markets.

Besides being a better description of the beer, "Blonde" might actually mean something to beer drinkers. "Premium" was actually a term "manufactured" by the national brewers in the '60s and '70s. The idea was to position their beers as somehow better or higher quality than some of the regional offerings like Old Style, Lone Star and, of course, Shiner. The smaller brewers followed along with the big national brands and attached "premium" to their brews in an effort to remain relevant. Many of those regional brewers were eventually put out of business after the big brewers drove the price of their beers downward. Most of the little guys were unable to compete. Shiner, in fact, was one of the few to survive. The jettisoning of the "premium" label in favor of "blonde" was confirmation that Shiner had not only survived, but would play by its own rules, not those made by others.

The reintroduction proved helpful too. Sales rose substantially and served to strengthen an already impressive decade for the brewery.

In '99, Shiner celebrated its largest Bocktoberfest ever, with more than 17,000 Shiner fans making the pilgrimage and putting away their fair share of the Spoetzl Brewery's output while watching some of the best that Texas music had to offer.

The "G.A.S.P." (Great Austin to Shiner Pedal) bike ride that had started back in the '80s as a ride from Austin to Shiner transitioned into "B.A.S.H." (Bike Austin, San Antonio, Houston) offering still more tangible two-wheeled proof that the beloved "Austin beer" had indeed become the preferred

The weather coulda been better, but they managed to warm things up.

BOCKT

HOT TUNES ★

ROBERT EARL KEEN MARC[H]

RAY WYLIE HUBBARD THE GREAT DIVIDE CLINT BLACK
KENNY WAYNE SHEPHERD

JUNIOR BROWN AUDIOSLAVE GOOD
HARR[Y]

ASLEEP AT THE WHEEL UGLY AMERICANS COLL
TRIS

THE FABULOUS THUNDERBIRDS JESSIE GUITAR TAYLOR MONTE

BUGS HENDERSON THE HOLLISTERS THE DEAD CRICKETS KELLY

CAROLYN WONDERLAND ZYDECO DOTS MAX STALLING DE

JACK INGRAM ROGER CREAGER BILL PEKAR THREE DAYS GRACE K

BLUE OCTOBER SOULAR SIDE PAT GREEN
SEETHER

KEVIN FOWLER THE DERAILE[R]
OLD 97'[S]

STEPHANIE URBAN JONES ERIC JOHNSON
JACKOPIERCE TODD SNIDER

OBERFEST

COLD BEERS

BALL   FONDUE MONKS   DIAMOND RIO   THE MIGHTY MIGHTY BOSSTONES
HUGH FADAL BAND

LOST IMMIGRANTS   JERRY JEFF WALKER
PATRICE PRICE   CORRY MORROW

HARLOTTE   STAIND   IAN MOORE   TONI PRICE
& RYDEN   GEORGE DEVORE & THE ROAM
TIVE SOUL
MURPHY   CHARLIE ROBISON   JOHN W. PRICE & THE WRONG WAY BAND

TGOMERY   REV. HORTON HEAT   SHEDAISY   RANDY ROGERS BAND
ILLIS   LYLE LOVETT
TITO & TARANTULA
RT McCLINTON   SKUNKWEED

ROCK   RECKLESS KELLY   GODSMACK   JOE ELY
ARRYL LEE RUSH   NICKELBACK   TRAPT
ERRI HENDRIX   IAN MOORE

S CROSS   & FIREWORKS!
ANADIAN
RAGWEED

home brew of the entire state. Some guy named Lance most likely had something to do with the popularity of the bike ride. The fact that he enjoyed a cold Shiner Bock now and again, made it even better.

As the long lines of cyclists rode into town, some of the domino players in the back rooms of the little stores made their way outside to take in the sight of it all. There might have been a comment or two about the tight shorts and the bright jerseys, but mostly there was appreciation of the fact so many other people from so many other places loved what they loved. Moreover, their town mattered. They'd always known that, of course, but it was gratifying nonetheless that so many other people, strange clothing or not, felt that it mattered too.

And as the century came to a close and people most places worried about whether their computers would go haywire in the new millennium and if the lights would still work or if there'd be some kind of Y2K meltdown at the stroke of midnight, the folks in Shiner took it all in stride. They'd lived through two world wars and Prohibition and a whole lot of other battles that didn't have names, and yet the old brewery had always kept going. And so it would continue too, as the 19s turned into the two thousands. The old place had taken every-thing that had been thrown at it and survived. Now, it was doing more than that while at the same time, through the brew it produced, harkening back to a different time most people can only read about.

It's a story that would ring of overdone fiction if it weren't for the simple fact the whole damn thing's true. It did happen and, in fact, is still happening, thank you very much. And outside the confines of some imaginative writer's mind, there is only one place it could have all come about, and that is here. This country was, and is, after all, a place built by immigrants. And to anyone who has ever visited, there is surely no place more American and, more specifically, Texan than Shiner.

That an immigrant had started the whole thing in the first place was as it should have been. That an immigrant now would take it into the next millennium was all the better still.

A new herd out on the brewery grounds: Can you say, "Voodstock?"

138

Rock star and Brewmaster Jimmy Mauric pumps up the crowd with a toast.

A fitting end to a great day: Fireworks over the brewhouse.

★ CH. 9 ★

JUST WAIT 'TIL

WE AGE

THIS THING A LITTLE BIT MORE!

LOOKING FORWARD TO THE NEXT 100 YEARS OR SO

2000 TO 2009

Has Shiner been specially blessed? Yes, I think you'd have to say it is true. This fact, of course, should never be confused with the notion that things have always gone their way. They have not. Joseph, of Old Testament fame, was specially blessed, yet endured innumerable hardships en route to the full realization of said blessings.

An unromanticized look at the life, times and struggles of the Spoetzl Brewery, from its improbable beginnings to its brinks of failure and on around to its very nearly fairy-tale endings confirms that "blessing" in no way equals a ride without bumps.

But however happy things may now be, we haven't reached the ending anyway, have we? No...And there may well be travails of which we can have no inkling lurking off in the future. Still, the likelihood of surviving said travails is now greater than it ever was. Yes, the arrival of the K. Spoetzl Brewery at the doorstep of the 21st century was something that more than once seemed very much in doubt, but that's the fun thing about special blessings. Often as not, they remain unseen until such time as the need for the improbable comes along.

Will it always be so? About this, we can only speculate. The early returns look good, though. The "microbrewery" craze, as crazes are inclined to do, came and went, buoying many a little brand to cult status for a brief, heady time. Certainly Shiner benefited a good deal from it, especially in places where it hadn't been marketed before. Certainly the timing of the renewed marketing efforts was a blessing, given all that. But you'd be shortsighted were you to simply attribute the near-miracles of the last couple of decades to a "craze." Many of the darling little brands of that time found themselves on hard times once the novelty wore off and the hype of the microbrewery thing abated.

Shiner, having been a "microbrewery" long before it was cool and even before there was such a word, was not a phenomenon of that time and therefore didn't suffer to the extent many others did when it all came back to earth. Back at the brewery in Shiner, where feet tend to stay planted firmly on Planet Earth, there were smiles of disbelief and the shaking of heads at the oddities of popular culture and the fact that you can become suddenly "cool" without doing so much as a single thing different than you've always done.

Awards or not, humility, like pure artesian water, was always going to be one of the main ingredients of the beer made down on Brewery Street. That's why, when there was much uncertainty about whether or not to come out with a light beer, the brewery turned not to focus groups or product consultants. They instead enlisted the people of Shiner to tell them which way to go.

In the summer of '03, the brewery asked everybody in town—matter of fact—everybody in the entire 77984 zip code to come to a special party at the brewery. Nobody was told the purpose of the gathering—just that Shiner was unveiling a new brew, subject to the approval of the townspeople. Rumors ran rampant about just what the new offering might be. Light beer was generally far down the list of guesses as most folks thought it to be strictly the province of the big brewers and therefore somewhere Shiner would never tread.

On the day of the party, much to the surprise of most, Shiner introduced Shiner Light. Everyone was given a chance to try it and either endorse it or give it the thumbs down. The new Shiner Light was overwhelmingly approved and put on the fast track to general distribution. Here, of course, you'd be excused if you asked what would have happened had they not liked it. Quite simply, the answer is "nothing." If the majority hadn't approved, it would have been back to the drawing board and then down the road somewhere there probably would have been another party—something nobody around Shiner ever seems to have much of a problem with anyway.

The key was involving the whole town. The Spoetzl Brewery has always been an important part of the town of Shiner, but over some of the years, when the brewery was just barely alive, that focus was inward. The big Shiner Light Approval party was a way to make certain the brewery remained true to its roots, while thanking the townspeople who'd supported them through thick and thin.

I suppose it goes without saying that there aren't too many places where they still do things that way, but I've said it anyway and I will say it some more in another chapter. Even then, there will be no worry on my part about over-emphasis, for Shiner truly is a most un-ordinary place—one that stands out even more these days, given the sameness of a world in which the electronics outlet and hardware megastore on the corner give you no clue as to whether you are in Houston, Texas or Buffalo, New York. When you are in Shiner, you will know.

Blessings.

There's the artesian well they found there after digging a mere 55 feet. There's the man from Bavaria who blew improbably into town and chose this place after trying just about every other town on the face of the planet. There are the people who came to work there as teenagers and stayed till their 80s. The revenue agent who turned his head during Prohibition, so long as there was always a batch of the "real stuff" waiting for him. Certainly, and most importantly, there are the people that drank the beer and drink it still, not to mention the many more that may not have yet discovered it.

And if we are to make an accounting of blessings received and yet to come, surely chief among them would be that one for which we all strive...long life. 100 years of life, be they allotted to a man, woman, or institution, certainly deserve celebration and thanksgiving. In 2005, the brewery began, quite literally, counting its blessings, down to the day it would reach its centennial. Shiner '96 (for the 96th year of the brewery) became the first of five annual commemorative brews. 96 was a Märzen-style Ale. Shiner 97, released in 2006, was a Bohemian Black Lager. In 2007, Shiner 98, a Bavarian Style Amber debuted. 2008's Shiner 99 is a Munich-style Helles. Shiner 100, of course, will be introduced to coincide with the brewery's centennial.

Kosmos Spoetzl, though he would probably loathe such fancy titles as "consultant," certainly could have properly been given that rank in the creation of all these anniversary beers. It may have been 59 years since we enjoyed the smell of his cigars, the squeaky old shocks of his Ford Coupe, or the jingling change in his big pockets, but we never lost track of his heavily accented voice. That his and the Spoetzl Brewery's Czech/German heritage are a very tangible part of these special beers is certainly no accident.

Blessings never are.

Humility, like pure artesian water, was always going to be one of the main ingredients of the beer made down on Brewery Street.

PAID AT THE RATE PRESCRIBED BY INTERNAL REVENUE LA...

CONTENTS 12 FLUID ...

Shiner Beer

SHINER

LA...
B...

MADE ONLY FROM
Fancy Malt

and Choice...

...TZL BREWERY

SHINER, T...

L ike any 100-year-old, Shiner didn't always look like it does now. They've added a few wrinkles here or there along the way. Here, a look back on the younger years.

Seeing as it's not every day you hit a hundred, Shiner has made sure to make the celebration last as long as possible. They got the party started a little early, back in '05, with Shiner 96. Every year, it's been a different limited-edition brew, to take us all right up to the big year. Here's to triple digits.

BEER BREAK

We could talk all we want about Shiner, but sometimes, the best things are what Shiner drinkers say. Over the years the folks at Shiner have collected quite a nice little stack of love letters, photos from all over the world, plus a song or two. They've even got a whole bunch of beloved pets named after the beer. One, in particular, is worth retelling here. Brandon Wulz of Dallas adopted a 10-week-old puppy back in 1995 and decided to name him after his favorite beer. That, of course, was the easy part. Beyond the naming part of owning a puppy was the dog-walking, the whining and the chewing-things-up part. So it was that after little more than a month of dog ownership, Brandon decided to return Shiner to the SPCA.

On the way there, he passed a billboard for Shiner Bock. It was a sign both in the literal and the figurative sense. Somebody was telling him something. Brandon turned around and took Shiner back home with him. The two of them remained inseparable until Shiner's passing in 2008.

Who says advertising doesn't make a difference?

A cold Shiner Black Lager shot in Ginny's Little Longhorn in Austin, Texas.

Customer Relations
Spoetzl Brewery
Shiner, Tx   77984

To the Decision Makers at the Brewery;

    First off I'd like to state that I am a native Texan, state loving, and avid enjoyer of ya'lls beer. Both the Premium and the Bock are absolutely delicious. I do not drink just to drink and I am not one of the many yuppies on the night clubbing, drinking to get smashed, faddish Shiner bock beer craze. I drink Shiner because I truly enjoy the taste of the beer. My dad drank Shiner when it wasn't damn near $5.00 dollars a six pack. Now, I am an educated man, college graduate and understand about supply and demand and the economics of business and the nature of the faddish beast. Ya'lls beer was great for so long and still is, but there are more complaints on my part today than there are compliments. This is a shame since I was such an ambassador and advocate for ya'lls beer before all the changes.

    The complaints on my part start with the changing of the label. This new label with it's red colored bock emblem, less distinguished ram and it's absence of the ever so famous quote, "SPECIALLY BREWED FOR THE DISCRIMINATING BEER DRINKER BY THE LITTLE BREWERY IN SHINER", which appealed to small town Texas folk all over the state. It appealed to me! I use to say with friends that this is my favorite beer not only for the taste but for this little quote in red here at the bottom of the bottle! Please change the label back and ignore the uprise of the faddish yuppie drinking, senseless paying $5.00 a six, youthful generational appeal kick which ya'll seem to be on. Just for ya'lls information I am twenty five years old and that this statement is not coming from an old timer against all youthful generation advancements.

    My next complaint is this new Shiner Honey Wheat. I tried it here in San Marcos where I live at the time, at a nice place and absolutely, thoroughly thought it was not a great idea on ya'lls part. It had an undeniably wrongful citrus taste and in my opinion and I feel it hurt ya'lls reputation as a lover of small town Texans. Now as I stated before I understand business and companies' striving for profit through diversification but this beer is an injustice to ya'lls name.

    My last complaint is that ya'll do not give tours on Saturday. My cousin, who is another enjoyer and I have long wanted to come visit yall and take a tour but have not for this reason. We are both working men and work all week and therefore are not able to make a weekday tour, but would be able and pleased to enjoy one on Saturday.

    These are my opinions that I feel are not only valid but should be addressed by ya'll. Shiner beer is a pleasurable way to sooth the thirst of a dry, parched throat and palate at the end of a hard day and I'd like ya'll to take that into consideration after ya'll read this letter. I will continue to drink Shiner when the funds are available and I will keep enjoying the taste of the Bock and the Premium but wanted to state the points above!

    I appreciate ya'lls time and would greatly appreciate a response from ya'll.

Sometimes your best
fans can also be your
biggest critics.

Sincere and Concerned

P. Kevin Shepherd

P. Kevin Shepherd,

2/16/93

MR. JOHN HYBNER
BREWMIESTER
SPOETZL (SHINER) BREWERY
SHINER, TX 77984

Dear Mr. Hybner;

Please allow me to identify myself as a real beer lover and a long time fan of Shiner Bock. THANK YOU

Any Shiner beer fan had terror struck in his/her heart with this gentleman associated with Corona bought the Shiner operation. Corona isn't even a decent "near beer" but anything can be sold in the U.S. market with enough hype.

Over the past year I have detected some subtle changes in the taste of Shiner Bock and I have experienced some headaches not typically associated with pure brewed beers. There are rumors on the street that Shiner has gone to using corn syrup instead of barley malt in order to increase its production and sales. Is this true? Maybe you can't answer that for various reasons. But you could assure me that Shiner contains only the finest barley malt, hops and yeast as you once so proudly advertised.

I can't help but notice that you seem to have dropped the pure approach to brewing from your advertisement.

It would really be a shame if someone from a synthetic beer background like Corona has seen fit to impose a change on the rich traditional brewing methods of Shiner.

Shiner is part of this state's heritage and hopefully you are guarding that precious resource every day.

Sincerely,

John P. Walter

BREWERS' ASSOCI

EXECUTIVE SECRETARY

WILLIAM M. O'SHEA

541 W. RANDOLPH ST.

TELEPHONE AREA CODE 312

STATE 2-2306

CHICAGO, ILLINOIS 60606

DEDICATED TO THE BEST INTERESTS OF THE BREWING INDUSTRY

October eighteenth
1 9 7 6

LET US GIVE THANKS!

The President of the United States signed H.R. 3605.

The bill provides that the Excise Tax on Beer shall be reduced
from $9 to $7 a barrel - on the first 60,000 barrels produced
by a Brewer in a year - provided the Brewer produces no more
than 2,000,000 barrels a year.

Glory, Glory Hallelujah,

William M. O'Shea
Executive Secretary
Brewers' Association of America

WOS:grs

CAUGHT WITH BOCK

FROM A FEW OF OUR FRIENDS

Whether it's drinking Shiner at the beach or in the shower, decorating the Christmas tree or a Halloween costume, it's safe to say that Shiner's made it into not just the gullets, but the hearts of plenty. Back in '03, Shiner asked folks to submit their favorite memories of Bock in order to win a simple contest. SIX years later and they're still coming in. The folks down in Shiner don't mind though. In fact, they say, "keep 'em coming."

LETTERS FROM A FEW OF OUR FRIENDS

BETSY REESE

"I, Betsy Reese, was having lunch with my mother at the Grist Mill in Gruene, TX, several years ago. We both ordered Shiner Bock. As I took a big swig of my beer I felt something in my mouth. I spit it in my hand...it was a dead fly. My mother asked if I wanted another beer. I declined as the fly was dead and the beer was sterile, alcohol of course, and continued our lunch. I saw no need to bother the waiter. My mother, now deceased, started me on beer at a very young age as she thought cokes were not healthy. I have consumed beer all over the world but always come back to Shiner Bock! Sad to say if this had happened to some yuppie liberal they would have had to have a lawyer involved. At 73 years of age I hope to continue enjoying your brew. Just another funny thing...earlier this month in Temple, TX, at the Duck Tavern we were with friends and lucked onto their Happy Hour. A first-night waitress took our order for beers at a dollar per bottle. My order for Shiner Bock was not included as it was IMPORTED. I said, 'Oh no, it was brewed in this great state.' So, drank a few at a dollar...such a deal!"

BILL PRATHER

"In 1973, we were visiting San Antonio for Christmas. We were living at the time in Salt Lake City. We have numerous relatives in Gonzales and had been visiting with them when my grandmother decided to make a trip to the brewery. Upon arriving there, we sat down at a table in the sampling room (I believe that is where it was). She ordered a pitcher of beer for herself and a pitcher of beer for the rest of the table. She created many fans for life that day.

ED SULLIVAN

"So I was sitting at a bar in Austin about 20 years ago when a Shiner delivery man came in and sat along side me. I don't remember what I was wearing, but it had to be some type of interesting shirt. Anyhow, the delivery guy was wearing a Shiner shirt with his name on it—Ed. It also happens to be my name. After a few more Shiners, we switched shirts there at the bar.

I still have the shirt and wear it whenever I am in a Shiner kind of mood. It is one of my most prized possessions."

CHAD LOUP

"While studying at UT I was fortunate enough to witness Vince's Rose Bowl winning national championship touchdown in 2005. After the victory, everything is a blur except for one moment I will never forget. We all ran to the Drag and I bought a T-shirt at the Co-Op. Within seconds after putting it on, someone gave me a Shiner Bock in the street and I was so pumped I decided to wear the beer on my new shirt. To this day every time I put it on I want to drink a Shiner. I will always remember that moment.

JOHN SPREEN

"When I was a young boy (I'm about to turn 61) I would ask my father why he drank Shiner and he would always say that it was doctor recommended. He said that his doctor told him that if you are going to drink beer, it might as well be Shiner.

We keep Shiner Light in the beer box at all times because it is without a doubt the best tasting light beer on the market. It is more like a microbrew than a light beer.

Keep the hops a hopping."

ERIC BRACH

"Back in January of '06 I was living in Washington, DC. Though I found myself up north, I was seeing a girl from Texas; being the good southern folk that we were, one of the things we had in common was a love for the mellow taste of a nice, cool Shiner Bock.

Texas was playing USC in the college football national championship back then, and the two of us met up at a bar to watch the game. We wanted to bet on it, of course; thing was, neither of us would take USC. So we set up something special.

If Texas won by 7 or less, she'd buy me a six-pack of Shiner. If Texas won by more than a TD, well, I'd have to buy her a whole case. If Texas lost, we agreed we'd call it a wash and just drown our sorrows together.

Well, UT came back from twelve points down to win 41-38, and danged if I didn't win myself a six-pack of Shiner. That girl and I have long since stopped seeing each other, but I'll always have the sweet, sweet taste of ice cold Shiner to remember her by."

BRAD HORN

"Simply put...I love Shiner Bock. I left Texas in 2000 after my first 25 years of life as a Texan. Though I have found happiness here with my career and my personal life, the absence of the availability of Shiner in central New York state is brutally painful. The Austin airport used to sell Shiner in the gift shop, which would allow me to stuff a couple of six packs in my back pack on my way home, but alas, that practice has been suspended."

CASPER

"I can still remember being able to buy beer right out of that place from the night watchman before the laws got strict. Boy those were the good ole days."

AMY OTHOLD

"I grew up in Columbus, TX, and attended The University of Texas in Austin. I began dating Reg Othold, a native of Shiner, TX, who was attending Texas A&M University. When Reg went to Columbus to meet my parents, my Dad told him a story that I had heard before, but had new significance since I was now dating someone from Shiner. My father, Arthur Evans, Jr. attended The University of Texas in the 1940's. He was returning to Austin one Sunday after visiting his parents in Columbus. It was a very cold and rainy day. He came across an older man on the side of the road. His vehicle had a flat tire. My father stopped and changed the tire for him. It turned out that this was Mr. Spoetzl. He asked my father questions about who he was, what he was studying, what fraternity he belonged to and where he lived in Austin. He was very grateful for my Dad's assistance. About a week later, my Dad received a phone call from a gas station near him in Austin. He was told that a case of Shiner beer had been left there for him, and he should come to pick it up. My Dad went to the station to get the beer. The owner explained that Mr. Spoetzl had sent it in appreciation of my Dad's help on the side of the road that cold day. He explained that my Dad was to return the empties the following week. My Dad and his friends drank the beer and he returned the empties to the station. Imagine his surprise when there was another case of beer there for him. This went on for an entire year! Mr. Spoetzl apparently was not only grateful, but was exceedingly generous in showing his appreciation."

Joe Patek of the Joe Patek Orchestra in Shiner: One of the more famous Czech/German polka bands in Texas.

PROSIT!

GREAT BEER DESERVES GREAT MUSIC.
Here are a couple of favorites played regularly by the Joe Patek Orchestra of Shiner, Texas.

THE SHINER SONG

Když jsme opustili Shiner, slunce svítilo.

Když jsme opustili Shiner, slunce svítilo.

Piva bylo dosti, a jídla do sytosti.

Piva bylo dosti, a jídla do sytosti.

Když jsme opustili Shiner, slunce svítilo.

Když jsme opustili pivovar, bečka byla prázdná.

Když jsme opustili pivovar, bečka byla prázdná.

A my jsme popíjeli, a dobře jsme se měli.

A my jsme popíjeli, a dobře jsme se měli.

Když jsme opustili pivovar, bečka byla prázdná.

Když jsme opustili Prahu, slunce svítilo.

Když jsme opustili Prahu, slunce svítilo.

Piva bylo dosti, a jídla do sytosti.

Piva bylo dosti, a jídla do sytosti.

Když jsme opustili Prahu, slunce svítilo.

When we left Shiner, the sun was shining.

When we left Shiner, the sun was shining.

There was plenty of beer, and lots of food.

There was plenty of beer, and lots of food.

When we left Shiner, the sun was shining.

When we left the brewery, the barrels were empty.

When we left the brewery, the barrels were empty.

And we were drinking and having a good time.

And we were drinking and having a good time.

When we left the brewery, the barrels were empty.

When we left Prague, the sun was shining.

When we left Prague, the sun was shining.

There was plenty of beer, and lots of food.

There was plenty of beer, and lots of food.

When we left Prague, the sun was shining.

KRÁSNÁ AMERIKA

Krásná to je krásná, to je krásná Amerika.

V Americe tam je blaze, tam teče pivo po podlaze.

Krásná to je krásná, to je krásná Amerika.

Proto se všichni sejdeme, do Ameriky pojedeme.

Krásná to je krásná, to je krásná Amerika.

Krásná to je krásná, to je krásná Amerika.

V Americe jsou slepice, ty nesou vejce jak čepice.

Krásná to je krásná, to je krásná Amerika.

Proto se všichni sejdeme, do Ameriky pojedeme.

Krásná to je krásná, to je krásná Amerika.

Beautiful, yes it's beautiful, it's our beautiful America.

In America there is everything grand.

Beautiful, yes it's beautiful, it's our beautiful America.

Good folks, good beer, it's always on hand.

Beautiful, yes it's beautiful, it's our beautiful America.

Beautiful, yes it's beautiful, it's our beautiful America.

In America we're happy to be.

Beautiful, yes it's beautiful, it's our beautiful America.

To work, to plan, and to know that we're free.

Beautiful, yes it's beautiful, it's our beautiful America.

CHAPTER TEN

MAYBERRY WITH A GERMAN ACCENT

Outside the realities of Santa and the Easter bunny, maybe one of the greatest disappointments of my pre-adolescent life was the disturbing news that the *Andy Griffith Show's* town of Mayberry was actually just a Hollywood backlot set. They'd done such a great job of recreating a little southern town and its oddball characters, I'd bought into it all, hook, line and even the sinker hanging off the end of Opie's cane fishing pole.

So I guess, it was with some trepidation that I made my first trip to Shiner. All I'd read and heard from people who'd been there seemed way too good to be true. I figured I'd get there and find the quaintness to be prefabricated in a Chamber of Commerce tourism book kind of way and end up having to file it away with Mayberry and the Tooth Fairy.

A friend of mine out of Austin who'd helped plan the surprise party introduction of Shiner Light to the townspeople of Shiner a few years ago, told me a story about the place in an effort to let me know what to expect. He rolled into town late one morning and stopped at Howard's convenience store on the edge of town. While in there, he noticed a flyer for a local musician in town. My friend enquired of the storeowner as to whether he knew the singer and whether he might be interested in playing at a little party in a few weeks. The storeowner said he'd check into it, and my friend left his number and headed on down the road.

A couple minutes later, at a barbecue place on the other end of town, my friend again pulled in and enquired as to whether they did catered meals. The barbecue joint owner looked up and said, "Oh, you must be the guy having the big party I heard about." A grand total of maybe ten minutes had elapsed since my Austin friend had hit the city limits and his "secret" mission was already the subject of chatter from one end of town to the other. Were it not for the fact the *Shiner Gazette* only comes out once a week, there would have already been an article in there as well.

Everybody knows everybody in Shiner. This, of course, can be a good thing or a bad thing, but given the anonymity of most neighborhoods these days, it is, for the most part, a good thing. If the keeping of secrets is high on your list of priorities, I might suggest somewhere else, but if a glimpse into what small towns used to be like is of interest to you, Shiner's your place.

Unlike a lot of small towns in Texas, it is what it was. For the most part anyway. Certainly, it was once a big cotton-producing town. Over the years, that went by the wayside for a number of reasons, but there were other important things that didn't change. A look at the town paper gives you one insight as to why this is so. Notice the names. Patek, Boehm, Vavricka, Goeman, Heimann, Hodanek. Many of the Germans and Czechs who came here all those years ago, for whatever reason, never moved on to the bigger cities. Walk into any of the stores or restaurants and you're likely to encounter another oddity. The appearance of the folks would suggest you could be in any little town in Texas, but then you start up a conversation...Not always, but a lot of times, especially in the older ones, there's still just a little lilting hint of the old country in their accents. Some can even go from a slight Texas twang into faintly remembered German or Czech that a grandfather or aunt spoke around the house.

This is, of course, not to say there aren't folks of Hispanic, African-American, Irish and Scottish descent. There are. And in the town and at the brewery, you'll see the same mishmash of people and cultures you see anyplace else. It's just that here the main ingredient in the stew's more noticeable than in other towns.

Certainly, time has not stood still here, so I'll avoid the use of that overworked notion, but some of the decaying aspects of modern life in regard to the small town have been less virulent here. Family and valued heritage account for a lot of that, but there are more practical considerations as well. Most notably, there is work to be had in Shiner, a blessing many small Texas towns have lost over the years.

You might be surprised to know that the brewery is nowhere near the largest of those employers. That title falls to the Kaspar Wire Works, across the road, where they make, as you might expect, things out of wire.

They actually got their start making odds and ends out of the discarded wire from old fences—yes, the same fences Mr. Spoetzl used to leave his beers on back in the day. Anyway, the turning of the old and discarded into the new and usable was not a "cause" back when the Kaspar family started their enterprise; it was simply a way to make a living. Yet like their neighbors at Spoetzl, who would later become popular with the hippies for using only natural ingredients, the Kaspars were cool

football games...the mascot, you might be surprised to learn, is the "Comanches." You might ask about how that came to be too, while you're at it. I suppose that's because Comanches sound a whole lot fiercer than say, the "Fightin' Brewmasters." No doubt, there are also rules about the usage of mascots related to alcohol; still it's fun to think about what might have been.

Which leads me to another little side street in Shiner. As wine is to Italians, so beer is to some Shinerites. By this, I mean it is not at all unusual for it to be a part of the noon meal and certainly supper. As a direct result of that, it is not uncommon to hear the folks in town tell you that they tasted their first Shiner at the age of six, or maybe 12, or as one lady put it, "when I was old enough to say, 'beer.'"

There is one gentleman who tells the story of being about 12 years old and waiting for the school bus one day. As luck would have it, Mr. Spoetzl, out on his daily rounds, noticed the boy and pulled his old Ford Coupe over to offer the boy a ride to school. Knowing, as everyone did, who Mr. Spoetzl was, the ride was not being offered by a stranger and was thus gladly accepted. As they bounced down the road towards town, Kosmos asked the boy if he'd like a beer. Being headed towards

EVERYBODY KNOWS EVERYBODY IN SHINER.

...if a glimpse into what small towns used to be like is of interest to you, Shiner's your place.

way before anybody else had come up with the phrase "recycling."

In the purely economic sense, the wire works certainly has had the most impact on the town over the years.

And then there's the brewery. Certainly, unless you're a wire enthusiast or consumer of large numbers of gymnasium lockers, it's the place that put the town on the map. Most days in the summertime, 100 or more people show up there to take the tour and enjoy some complimentary beer in the Hospitality Room. You can easily spend a couple of hours there, but if you're headed that direction, allow yourself a little more time.

Maybe ask the tour guide about the rumors that during Prohibition there was an underground tunnel running under the road over to the wire works where a secret cellar allowed the Kaspars, at the end of a real hard day, to get themselves real cold beer. Ask about "The Shiner Song," the lyrics of which are in Czech and the melody is still played at the high school

the classroom, the boy demurred, but did reach around into the back of the old car and grab one for the old man.

I suppose these days we are supposed to shake our heads in disgust and wave an accusatory finger at such things as that—but again, this was another world from the one we know now.

It's hard, though, to feel too self-righteous or keep much of a scowl on your face when you roll past the "Cleanest Little Town In Texas" sign. If that doesn't do the job for you, maybe a stop at one of the local domino halls or a visit with the retired gentlemen who meet daily to call to order the latest session of the Shiner Beer Drinking Club will help you more effectively get into the vibe of this delightfully odd setting. Ask 'em to point out the brick in the town square they had inscribed and dedicated to "the unknown beer drinker." If you're lucky and hit town on a weekend, you might even get to hear the oompah music of the local "Hobo Band" down at the park.

Welcme To

SHINE

CLEANEST LITTLE CITY

HALF MOON HOLIDAYS 1ST

Driving into Shiner from Highway 92, this beautiful sign greets you from a nearby field. What's with the missing "o?", you ask? Well, I like to call that "character." Something you'll find plenty of in this little town.

Carrie Nation herself woulda been dancing on the tables had she ever the good fortune to come to this place.

Certainly cases have been made by many well-intentioned and not-so-well-intentioned souls over the years against the propriety of strong beverage. Yet even today, many in the medical profession have come around to the idea that in moderation there is good to be had from a daily beer or two, or maybe a glass of wine. Even this, of course, will never quiet the naysayers and the vehement teetotalers amongst us. But after a visit to this little town, even they would be given pause to soften the certainty of their views.

Unlike the beer named after it, Shiner, the town, is anything but cold.

Unofficial Town Greeter: Howard Gloor in the convenience store that bears his name, beers on tap and just about anything else you need.

167

Sam Schwartz ....Secretary
T. J. Burkett ..Marshall, Ass'r and Coll'r

LOCAL NEWS.

Cotton Receipts.

	BALES
Previously reported	1762
Received for week ending Aug. 28	1000
Total	2762

Market steady; average price, 12c.

—Window glass and putty at Schlottman Drug Co.

—The cotton seed war was also on in Shiner last week and seed went as high as $23 per ton.

—All kinds of legal blanks for sale at the Gazette office.

—Dr. Gus. Schulze is now riding in a fine new double seat auto, and he is very proud of his machine.

—Drink Shiner beer and you will laugh and grow fat.

—Mr. Frank Dolejsi went to Austin last week to have his eye treated, which was suffering from a bad injury.

—For fine eye-glasses and spectacles go to the Schlottman Drug Co.'s store.

—To parent and guardians: Don't forget that school will open on September 20, and have your children in readiness.

—If your eyes are troubling you, go to L. Gantert. A careful examination will cost you nothing

—Mr. Willie Tomasco is doing some nice work in painting and papering on the new residence of J. C. Habermacher.

—Ground bones are fine egg

—O. F. Schoenvogel and Anton Schilhab are new subscribers to the Gazette. They are both welcome.

—Mrs. Max Wolters was visiting relatives in San Antonio last week.

—A big stock of paints, oils varnishes and enamels at Schlottmann Drug Co

—Misses Lillie Wolters and Hilda Trautwein are visiting relatives and friends in Schulenburg.

—Try those ground bones at L. B. Richter's meat market. They will make your hens lay.

—Mrs. Ella Moeckel and daughter, Christie, returned Monday from a ten day's visit to relatives at San Antonio.

—The U. S. revenue inspector was in Shiner last Saturday to inspect the new brewery, and of course, found everything O. K. The brewing of beer will now be commenced at once.

—Judging by the bills allowed at the last session of the Commissioners' court, a great deal of road work is being done in the county. That is as it should be, and we hope they will keep up the good work.

—The Gazette is requested to announce that there will be an important meeting of the Bluecher Park Verein next Saturday, September 4, when business of importance will be transacted. A full attendance is requested.

—Mrs. J. A. Wolters and son,

For sale by all druggists.

—The teachers of the Shiner public schools are requested to meet at the school house on Saturday, September 18, at 4 o'clock p. m.

—Mesdames E. J. Wangeman and H. A. Stuermer were visiting relatives and friends in Fayette and Colorado counties last week.

—Twenty new residences have been erected in Shiner during the past twelve months, and still there is a scarcity, not a vacant house in town.

—Mr. Chas. Duevel of Galveston, but formerly of Shiner, came in last week to visit friends. Charley thinks of returning to Shiner and will try farming.

—Mrs. Tommie Amsler arrived in the city last week on a visit to her mother and other relatives. Mrs Amsler makes her home at Ingram in Kerr county.

—Master Lawrence Fitzsimon, son of Dr. J. T. Fitzsimon of Castroville, who has been here visiting his fellow student, Mr. Francis Havel, returned to his home last Thursday.

—A real blessing to the afflicted is St. Nicodemus Laxative Chill Tonic. It cures Chills and Fever in one day. Money returned if it fails. Price 25c your druggist.

—Mrs. T. S. Hughes and daughter, Miss May, returned last week from an extended visit to relatives in California. They enjoyed their trip greatly but are pleased to get back to Shiner

police beat

LEFT: Local Shiner News from 1909.

RIGHT: Weekly Police Beat from 2003.

According to the pages of the *Shiner Gazette*, not much has changed in the last century in the small town.

Mon., 07/14/03, 8:59 a.m., Sgt. Berkman assisted Hallettsvi with an emergency call in Shiner.

Mon., 07/14/03, 10:46 a.m., Sgt. Berkman provided a funeral escort.

Mon., 07/14/03, 11:16 a.m., Sgt. Berkman assisted Shiner EMS with an emergency call.

Mon., 07/14/03, 1:05 p.m., Sgt. Berkman unlocked a vehicle for a local woman.

Mon., 07/14/03, 1:45 p.m., Sgt. Berkman took a frequent patrol request.

Tues., 07/15/03, 4:40 a.m., Res. Ptlm. Penley assisted Shiner EMS with a sick call.

Tues., 07/15/03, 11:30 a.m., Sgt. Berkman and Ptlm. Aguilar were called for a civil matter.

Tues., 07/15/03, 5:23 p.m., Res. Ptlm. Penley assisted Shiner EMS with a sick call.

Tues., 07/15/03, 8:10 p.m., Res. Ptlm. Penley was called for an alarm at a local business. The officer checked the location and found all to be secure.

Wed., 07/16/03, 7 a.m., Chief Brunkenhoefer assisted Shiner Fire Department with a report of a structure fire.

Wed., 07/16/03, 9:10 a.m., Chief Brunkenhoefer unlocked a vehicle for a local woman.

Wed., 07/16/03, 11:46 p.m., Res. Ptlm. Penley observed several suspicious individuals walking around the area of a local church. After identifying them, a security check of the church was made and an open door found. The location was thoroughly checked by the officer and the pastor, but nothing appeared to have been disturbed.

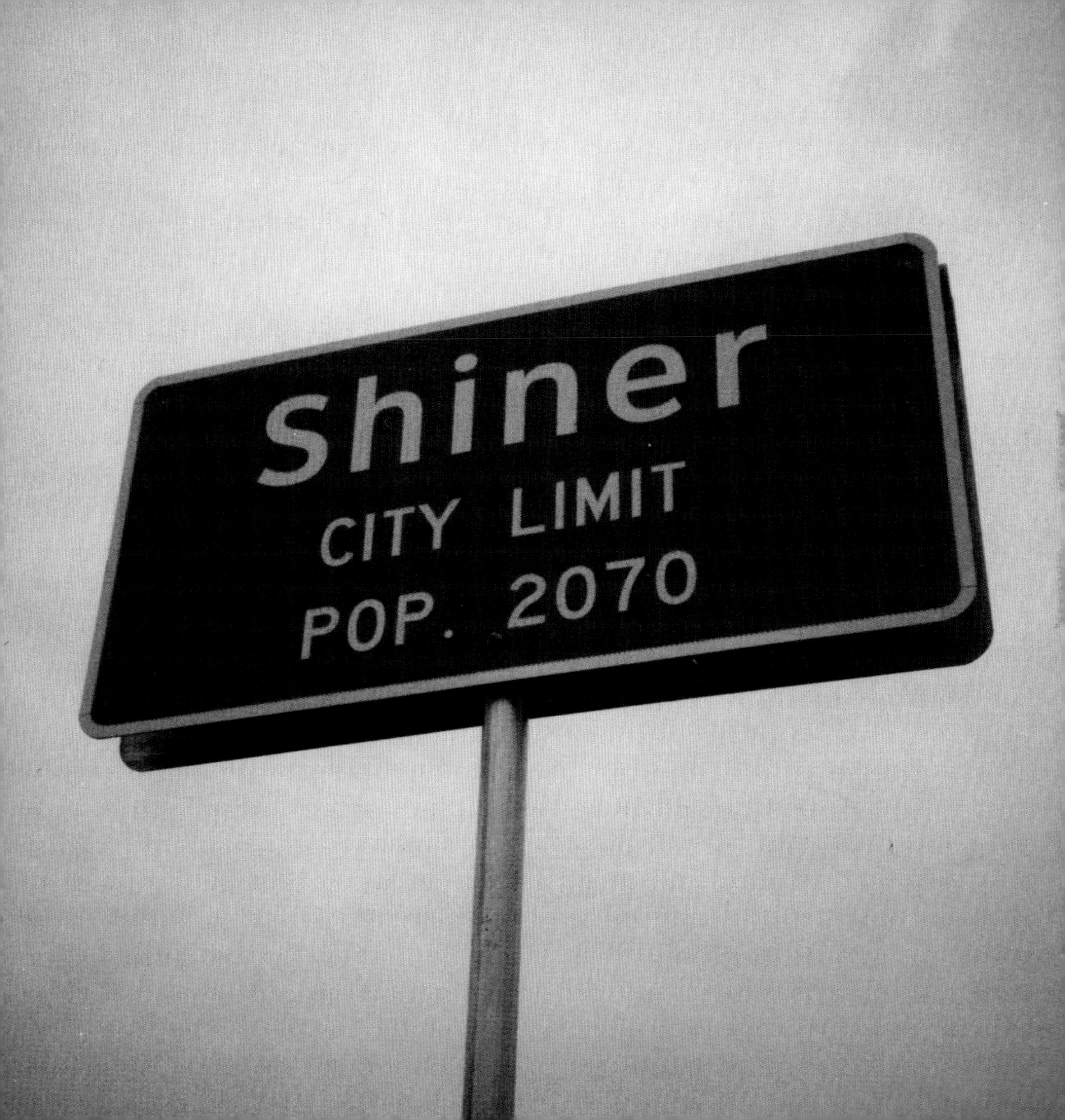
Shiner
CITY LIMIT
POP. 2070

BELOW: About as nice a next door neighbor as you'll ever have: Don Kaspar across the road at Kaspar Wire Works. Legend has it there's a tunnel under the highway from his place to the brewery.

RIGHT: Doing his part to conserve water: Shiner Fire Chief Emil Sembera supports the local brewery.

FROM TOP TO BOTTOM BY COLUMN:

The Old Farmer's COOP stood until 2008.

Wm. Green Building, downtown.

Texas Special Beer Wagon: equipped with kegs, taps and bar.

Shiner's local transit system.

Friday's: best fried chicken in Shiner.

Patek's Grocery Store: provides staples & butchered goods to Shinerites.

Opera House: ask for Ruth, what a gem.

Where all the town's gossip & news hits the press.

Old faithful: still flowing.

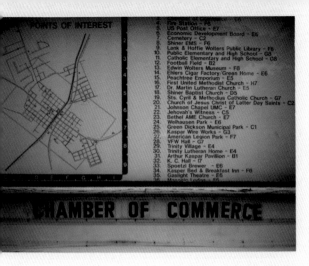  

Points of interest: outside of the E.H. Wellers Museum, run by Bernice.

Bernie runs the ol' museum at the Woelters's house; great guy.

Shiner's one and only traffic light.

The old Catholic church: small town cathedral.

Shiner's other major industry.

Wolter Brothers' department store, downtown.

Maeker's: best place to grab a sausage and a beer, ask for Martha.

Grab a chicken-fried steak at Werner's or buffet at Country Corner.

You are always welcome in this little town.

175

CHAPTER 11
WHO'S BEEN MESSIN' WITH MY SHINER?

Anonymity is both a blessing and a curse. Generally it's a blessing for those with tips for Crimestoppers and most anyone not particularly proud of their work. To those in search of a more human and humane world, as well as those who chase the dream of making art, anonymity's a dark and chilly thing.

Kosmos Spoetzl wore that hat kinda tilted on his head and drove around town in his unmistakable Ford Coupe with the washtub full of beers in the back because he wanted everybody to know who it was that made Shiner beer. It wasn't an ego thing or even grass-roots marketing, it's just that to Kosmos, beer was highly personal. He loved to see people drinking his beer and felt it only fair that those people should be able to see their beer being made. Moreover, he wanted everyone to know the people making it.

Certainly everybody knew Kosmos' namesake, Calvin Cosmo Wallace—Cracker—as you've come to know him already. For a good part of the 43 years he worked for the brewery, he drove the trucks that connected the beer lovers in Shiner with the beer lovers elsewhere. Appropriately enough, he was, perhaps, most famous in Austin. His big smile and good-natured laugh were looked forward to almost as much as the beer he brought. At Scholz' Garten, they always knew they could count on him to throw in a bunch of the Patek sausages along with his delivery.

Cracker drove pretty much every road in the state of Texas without incident until one day in the early '90s. There was a minor fender bender. He hadn't seen the other vehicle.

A subsequent eye exam deemed him to be legally blind.

Cracker was reassigned to the hospitality room and other duties around the brewery where he could engage in his new calling, sharing his endless stories about life out on the road and the early days with Kosmos. Even so, the relief at the thought of catastrophe avoided only partially tempered the sadness of an era ended.

No doubt Kosmos Spoetzl and his namesake had a good laugh about that one when he and Cracker were reunited. Calvin Cosmo Wallace passed away on June 9, 2002.

Today, there are 55 people who make the beer you drink. That's it. 55. Fewer people than may live on your block. It's hard to hide when there's only that many of you. And nobody here's interested in doing that anyway.

A lot of 'em are the second or even third generation to work at the brewery. Most grew up in town and never saw much need to go anywhere else. Certainly, most folks don't go anywhere else when they come to work at the brewery. Folks with 25, 35 years experience aren't hard to find at all. Cracker Wallace's father worked there well over half a century. The brewmaster, Jimmy Mauric, he's been there 30 years, starting from the bottom, unloading sacks of corn and hops at age 17, and working his way up.

One other thing you oughta know. Most everybody there has a nickname. A lot of times, the nickname—instead of the given name—will be stitched on their shirt.

Should you ever decide to come to work there, you might wanna come up with a good one for yourself before your first day. Otherwise, they'll come up with one for you whether you like it or not.

Funny thing, nicknames. Most people don't bother with them anymore. But if you think back to old days of big league baseball or the old *Our Gang* comedies, everybody had one. Maybe it's just the way times have changed or maybe we're just too sensitive these days to trouble with such things.

Rest assured, though, nobody's too sensitive on the floor of the K. Spoetzl Brewery. Unless, of course, you're talking about the beer. They take that real personally.

Red Bird

Rambo

Henrod

T-Bone

Stick

Chewy

LEFT: The King in his court: Herb Siems, presiding over the Hospitality Room, circa 1980.

RIGHT: Clockwise from top left: Calvin Cosmo Wallace, Elton Zander, Emil Grant and Joe Mack, circa 1980.

A SHORT LINEAGE OF BREWMASTERS

KOSMOS SPOETZL

1914-1950

GUS HASLBECK

1950-1966

WILLIAM BIGLER

1966-1968

CHESTER TERPINKSI

1968-1972

JOHN HYBNER

1972-2005

JIMMY MAURIC

2005-PRESENT

OUR FAMILY OF BEER LOVERS

GOOD THINGS COME FROM SMALL BREWERIES.

Chancey Baker, Racking Room, 3 years
Daniel Baker, Cellar, 3 years
Guadalupe Banda, Bottle Shop, 1 year
John Lee Bell, Maintenance, 13 years
Kirby Berckenhoff, Cellar, 1 year

Jeanette "Redbird" Boedeker, Janitor, 12 years
Elvis "T-bone" Brooks, Shipping/Supervisor, 15 years
Vans "Lucas" Carroll, Cellar, 3 years
Gregory "Everready" Coleman, Cellar/Asst. Supervisor, 27 years
Donald "Stick" Darilek, Bottleshop, 1 year

Robert "Bobby" Darilek, Maintenance Supervisor, 18 years
Anton Dews, Cellar, 8 years
Doris "Dotsy" Elliott, P.R./Hospitality, 12 years
Michael Fine, Cellar, 2 years
Christine "Tweety" Frederick, Maintenance, 1 year

   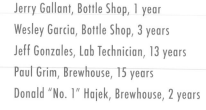 

Jerry Gallant, Bottle Shop, 1 year
Wesley Garcia, Bottle Shop, 3 years
Jeff Gonzales, Lab Technician, 13 years
Paul Grim, Brewhouse, 15 years
Donald "No. 1" Hajek, Brewhouse, 2 years

Richard Hartmann, Shipping & Receiving, 34 years
Zina Hartmann, P.R./Gift Shop, 6 years
Francisco "Frank" Hernandez, Racking Room, 2 years
Lester Hoepfl, Maintenance Engine Room/Supervisor, 39 years
Gregory Hybner, Assistant Brewmaster, 25 years

Linda Hybner, Lab Technician, 31 years
Clinton "C.J." Jahn, Truck Driver, 1 year
Otto Koliba, Maintenance, 1 year
Richard "Chewy"Koncaba, Bottle Shop, 2 years
Robert Koncaba, Bottle Shop, 8 years

Gail Kremling, Bottle Shop, 10 years
Donald Kurtz, Bottle Shop, 40 years
Byron Ludwig, Racking Asst. Supervisor, 13 years
Jimmy Mauric, Brewmaster, 30 years
"Sir" Charles McAfee, Brewhouse, 12 years

Kenny Michalec, Maintenance, 27 years
Amy Miller, Operations Coordinator, 1 year
Franklin Neubauer, Brewhouse, 14 years
Jeffery Parr, Bottle Shop, 1 year
Henry "Henrod" Pekar, Shipping & Receiving, 4 years

Anne Marie "Annie" Raabe, Public Relations, 8 years
Brent Rainosek, Bottleshop, 1 year
Ronnie "Rambo" Rainosek, Maintenance, 7 years
Patricia Schlenker "Pat", Office Receptionist, 8 years
Dorothy Schneider, Accounting Manager, 12 years

Peter Takacs, Lab QC Manager, 11 years
Lonnie "Chippy" Taylor, Truck Driver, 27 years
Kevin Tesch, Bottle Shop Supervisor, 12 years
Melissa Todd, Lab Technician, 1 year
Ray Turk, Maintenance, 13 years

Darrin "Bull" Wilson, Racking Room, 2 years
Gerald Zissa, Shipping & Receiving, 9 years

NOT PICTURED:
Timothy Molnoskey, Brewhouse, 8 years
Charles Moore, Shipping & Receiving, 1 year

BEER BREAK

LAST CALL

One last thing you should know. It's pronounced "Schpoetzl," not "Spetzl," or "Spotzl." This detail was one of the few non-beer-related topics that could get the old guy "to fussin'," as Cracker used to call Kosmos' half-English, half-German tirades. Tirade, given his personality, seems too harsh a word anyway and so I'll go with Cracker here and stick with "fussin'."

The things he fussed over the most are the things that you taste when you throw a bottle of his beer back and empty it of that wonderful liquid he put in there. He came to Shiner to make beer after trying to make it a half-dozen or so other places and, by God, after all that, he did.

I like to think that some part of our heavenly reward after we leave this earth is to look down upon that which we did and see what has become of it. Hopefully, he was spared the view during some of the more turbulent times, but is able now to see the place with his name still on the wall.

There is much that can't be known about the afterlife, though—that is, unless you get your ticket punched for the one-way ride there, so I'll stick to what I know about this life. Surely, it's been made better by Kosmos and all those who came along after him—people, who, like me, probably had a sneaking suspicion the old man was watching, and thus acted accordingly.

One other thing occurs to me: Kosmos' birth date. March 3. It was the day after Texas Independence Day. But upon further review, that was the date in Germany. In Texas, it was still Independence Day.

And in Shiner, it still is.

A cold Shiner Blonde shot out in the back of Howard's in Shiner, Texas.

LET US RAISE OUR GLASSES!

TO ALL OF YOU THAT MADE THIS BOOK AND THE LAST 100 YEARS OF SHINER BEERS POSSIBLE.

Henry B. Shiner	Bob Leggett	Ed Spradley
Kosmos Spoetzl	Marshall McHone	Travis Baker
Miss Celie	Rue Judd	Henry Billeck
Gus Haslbeck	Mark McGarrah	Brad Horn
William Biggler	Bryan Jessee	Chap Loup
Chester Terpinski	Chris Lowder	Peggy Mueller
Johnny Hybner	Brett Bunner	April
Jimmy Mauric	Craig Crutchfield	Erin Rourke
Joe Roller	Nicole Truly	Deborah Brown
Every Spoetzl Employee that has ever graced our brewery grounds.	Andrew Yates	Kenneth Groeschen
	Caroline Mowry	Martha Maeker
Carlos Alvarez	Mike Woolf	All of our fans and drinkers.
Charlie Paulette	Micael Priest	And anyone else we may have
Tess Liberto	Eddie Wilson	forgotten. You are in our hearts.
Anne Raabe	Phoebe Hunt	
The Old Geezers	B. Stratman	Kosmos knew pretty much all there
The Unknown Geezer	Gene Czora	was to know about brewing a great
The Kaspar Family	John Jennings	beer. But what he knew more than
Bernice	Pat McIntyre	anything, was that it was all for
Bernie Siegel	Betsy Reese	naught without good people to
Virginia Helweg	Susan Etheridge	make it and enjoy it.
Ruth Terpinski	John W. "Trey" Hancock III	
Howard Gloor	Bill Prather	And so it is still.
Frank Binney	Ed Sullivan	
Emil Sembera	Casper	With good friends like these,
Shiner Gazette Staff	John Spreen	100 years go by fast.
Michael Smith	Eric Brach	
Phil Vitek	Amy Othold	

Když jsme opustili Shiner, slunce svítilo.
Když jsme opustili Shiner, slunce svítilo.
Piva bylo dosti, a jídla do sytosti.
Piva bylo dosti, a jídla do sytosti.
Když jsme opustili Shiner, slunce svítilo.

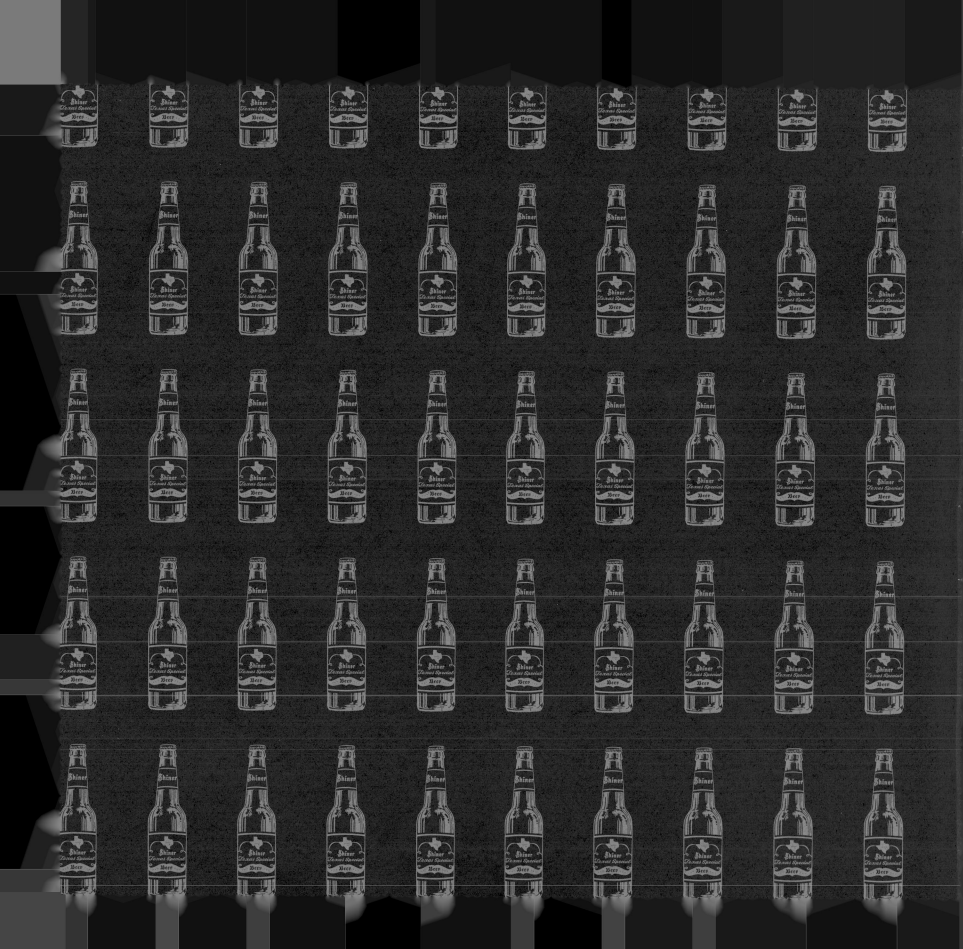